Critical **Grade 5**
& CREATIVE
Thinking Activities

Author: Rachel Lynette
Editor: Marilyn Evans
Copy Editing: Carrie Gwynne
Art Direction: Cheryl Puckett
Cover Illustration: Nathan Jarvis
Design/Production: Yuki Meyer

EMC 3395

Evan-Moor
EDUCATIONAL PUBLISHERS®
Helping Children Learn since 1979

Visit
teaching-standards.com
to view a correlation
of this book.
This is a free service.

***Correlated to State and
Common Core State Standards***

CONTENTS

What's in This Book? 4

Places

In the Woods 5
In a Cave 8
In the Desert.................... 11
In the Water 14
At the Ice-Cream Store 17
In the Kitchen................... 20
At a Party 23
At a Carnival 26
At a Museum 29
At a Garage Sale 32

Nature in Action

Ocean Life 35
Rain, Rain 38
Sunshine......................... 41
Snow Day! 44
Earthquakes and Volcanoes 47
Giant Squid 50
Bears 53
Dinosaurs........................ 56

Time to Eat

Time for Dessert! 59
Pizza 62
SSSlurp!......................... 65
School Lunch 68
Breakfast 71

Sports and Games

Play Ball! 74
It's All About Speed 77
Strikes and Spares............... 80
Board Games 83
Extreme 86

Things I Use

Shoes and Socks.................. 89
Spoons and Forks 92
Wheels 95
Remote Control 98
Money............................ 101
Water............................ 104

In My World

Light and Dark................... 107
Collections...................... 110
Sticks and Stones................ 113
Brothers and Sisters 116
Windows and Doors................ 119
Read All About It!............... 122
Screen Time...................... 125
Pets............................. 128
Giggles 131
Emotions 134
Choices 137
Homework 140

Answer Key 143

What's in This Book?

Critical and Creative Thinking Activities, Grade 5 contains 46 themes, each presented in a three-page unit that gives students valuable practice with a broad range of thinking skills. The engaging themes will keep students interested and will have them begging to do the next set of activities!

The first and second pages of each unit get students thinking about the topic in a variety of ways. They may be asked to draw on prior knowledge or to generate new ideas.

The last page of each unit features one of a number of stimulating and entertaining formats, including logic puzzles, riddles, and secret codes.

How to Use This Book

- Use the activity pages during your language arts period to keep the rest of the class actively and productively engaged while you work with small groups of students.

- The themed sets of activity pages provide a perfect language arts supplement for your thematic or seasonal units. And you'll find any number of topics that complement your science and social studies curricula.

- Your students will enjoy doing these fun pages for homework or as free-time activities in class.

About the Correlations for This Book

The valuable thinking skills practiced in this book (see inside front cover) are not generally addressed in state standards. However, thinking skills require content to be practiced. The activities in this book have been correlated to the Language Arts and Mathematics standards.

Visit www.teaching-standards.com to view a correlation of this book to your state's standards.

Sample Unit
Pages 86–88

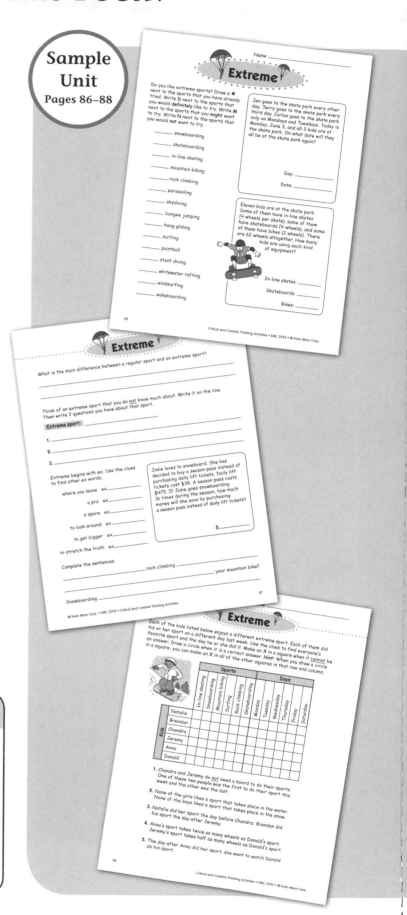

Critical and Creative Thinking Activities • EMC 3395 • © Evan-Moor Corp.

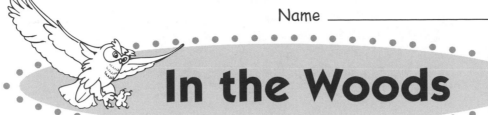

In the Woods

Name _____

Pretend that you are standing in the woods. What is...

the smallest thing you might see? _____

the most beautiful thing you might see? _____

the softest thing you might hear? _____

the softest thing you might touch? _____

the nicest thing you might smell? _____

ANAGRAMS

Rearrange the letters in each word to make the name of something you might find in the woods.

TAN _____

NOTES _____

FLEA _____

SLAIN _____

SENT _____

SNEAK _____

MASTER _____

Cory saw 27 animals in the woods.
Two-thirds of them were insects.
One-third of the insects were ants. The rest of the insects were flies. Cory saw two times as many squirrels as rabbits. Cory also saw a family of deer: a buck, a fawn, and a doe. How many of each animal did Cory see?

Ants: _____

Flies: _____

Squirrels: _____

Rabbits: _____

Deer: _____

Add adjectives and nouns to make the sentence more interesting.

We saw a bear in the woods.

_____

Name _____

In the Woods

What are 3 ways that spooky woods would be different from peaceful woods?

1. _____

2. _____

3. _____

SIMILES

The forest was as peaceful as _____.

The rabbit was as timid as _____.

The delicate wildflower was like _____.

Describe a tree to someone who has never seen one.

_____

_____

_____

There are 522 trees in Rachel's Woods. One-sixth of the trees are pine, one-third are fir, and half of them are cedar. How many of each kind of tree are in Rachel's Woods?

Pine: _____

Fir: _____

Cedar: _____

Woods is a synonym for *forest*.
Write a synonym for each word below.

quiet _____

beautiful _____

spooky _____

big _____

In the Woods

Read the clues and draw the trees where they belong.

 = tree

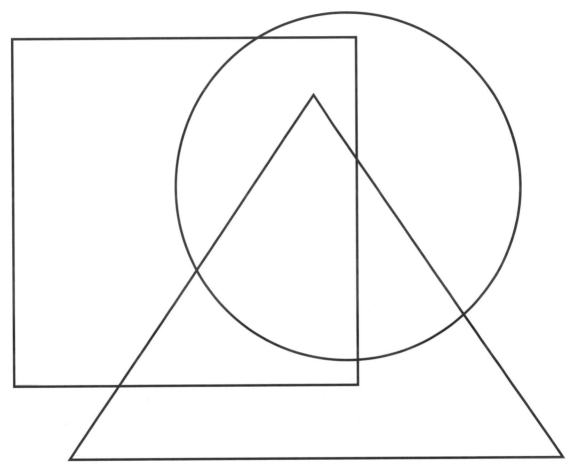

- There are 5 trees in only the square.

- There are 3 trees in only the triangle and the square.

- There are 6 trees in only the triangle.

- There are 2 trees in only the triangle and the circle.

- There are 4 trees in only the circle.

- There is 1 tree in only the circle and the square.

- There are 5 trees in all three of the shapes.

- There are 7 trees in none of the shapes.

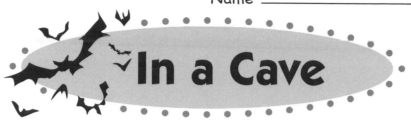

In a Cave

Would you like to explore a cave? _____

Why or why not? _____

_____

What are the most important things for a cave explorer to take on a caving expedition?
_____
_____
_____

What are some things other than rock formations that might be found inside a cave?
_____
_____
_____

Stalactites and stalagmites are cave formations made from dripping water that contains the mineral calcite. These formations form very slowly. Fill in the chart for each rate of growth to show how long a stalactite might grow over time.

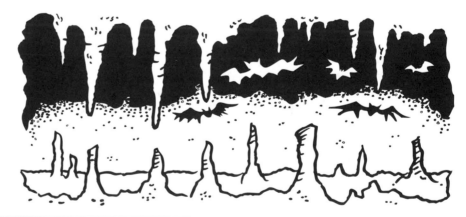

Rate of Growth	1,000 Years	20,000 Years	100,000 Years
200 years = 1 inch			
500 years = 1 inch			
2,000 years = 1 inch			
5,000 years = 1 inch			

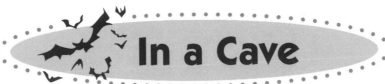

In a Cave

Add adjectives and adverbs to each sentence to make it more interesting.

The man crawled through the cave.

_____

Lucy saw stalactites in the cave.

_____

SIMILES

The cave was as dark as _____.

The cave was as quiet as _____.

The cavern was as big as _____.

Someone once asked a park ranger at Carlsbad Caverns National Park what was in the unexplored part of the cave. Why couldn't the park ranger answer the question?

_____

A syllogism is a kind of logical reasoning in which a conclusion is derived from the first two statements. Circle the letter of the statement that completes each syllogism.

All cave formations are delicate.
Stalactites are cave formations.
Therefore, _____.

A. some stalactites are delicate

B. all stalactites are delicate

C. all cave formations are stalactites

Some bats live in caves.
All bats are mammals.
Therefore, _____.

A. all mammals live in caves

B. all mammals are bats

C. some mammals live in caves

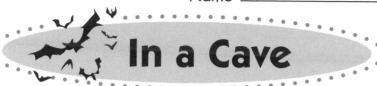

In a Cave

Can you get to the treasure and find your way out of the cave?

- Draw your path as you take one letter from each cavern to spell the word *TREASURE*.

- Circle the letter you take each time and write it on one of the lines below.

- You must take the letters in order.

- You may visit each cavern <u>only</u> once and you may <u>not</u> retrace your <u>own</u> path.

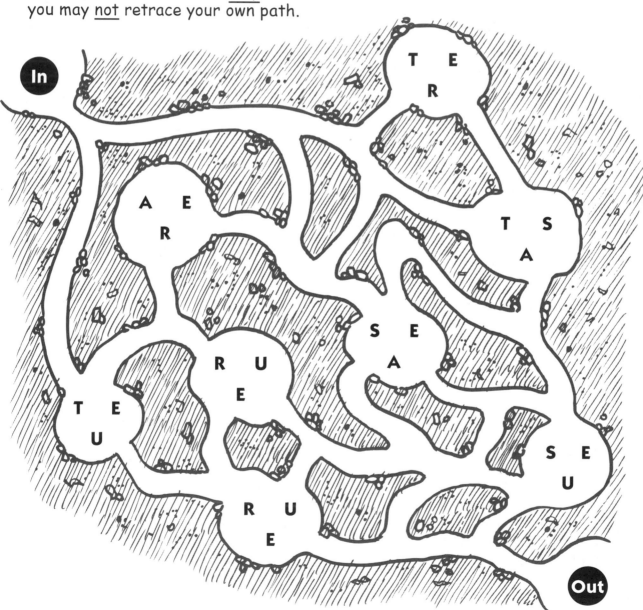

_____ _____ _____ _____ _____ _____ _____ _____

Critical and Creative Thinking Activities • EMC 3395 • © Evan-Moor Corp.

In the Desert

Name _____

You are going for a hike in the desert. You can take <u>only</u> 3 of the things listed below. Circle them.

water   snack

sand toys   sunblock

hat   sunglasses

snakebite kit compass

Joe's jeep can hold 25 gallons of gas in its tank, plus Joe has an extra tank that will hold another 25 gallons. His jeep can go 23 miles on 1 gallon of gas. He wants to cross a desert that is 1,200 miles long. Will Joe make it?

_____

A man is lost in the desert. He is out of water. He finds a water hole, but he does not drink from it. List 3 possible reasons.

1. _____

2. _____

3. _____

Circle the letter of the statement that completes each syllogism.

Some lizards live in the desert.
All lizards are reptiles.
Therefore, _____.

A. all reptiles live in the desert

B. some lizards are reptiles

C. some reptiles live in the desert

All deserts have little water.
The Sahara is a desert.
Therefore, _____.

A. the Sahara has little water

B. all deserts are the Sahara

C. all deserts have sand

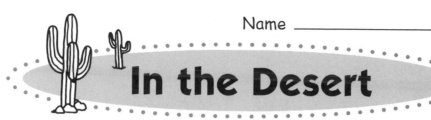

In the Desert

Use the clues to find things that are in a desert.

prickly plant   C_____

not really there   M_____

reptile   S_____

on the ground   S_____

stinging, spiderlike   S_____

reptile   L_____

What are 6 words that describe the desert?

1. _____

2. _____

3. _____

4. _____

5. _____

6. _____

Write a sentence that is always true about deserts.

_____

Write a sentence that is sometimes true about deserts.

_____

Write a sentence that is never true about deserts.

_____

DRAW IT:

• There are 3 cactus plants.

• The cactus in the middle is the tallest. The one on the left is smaller than the one on the right, which has 2 red flowers.

• There is a bird on the smallest cactus.

    Critical and Creative Thinking Activities • EMC 3395 • © Evan-Moor Corp.

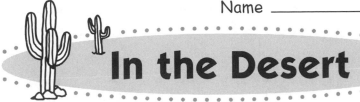

In the Desert

To get through the desert, you must follow the cactus trail. Draw a path that spells the word *CACTUS* again and again. You may go up, down, or to either side, but <u>not</u> diagonally. The trail starts with the **C** in the upper-left corner and ends with the **S** in the lower-right corner.

C	A	C	A	C			C	A	C	T	L	I	Z	A	R	D
A	K	T	P	T			S	J	L	Z	R	F	S	C	A	C
C	Y	U	M	U			U	S	C	A	C	T	U	P	K	T
T	W	S	C	A			T	W			P	S	M	V	U	
		G	C	P	U	Y	C	T			B	C	K	R	S	
		J	T	I	T	H	A	R			Z	A	L	A	C	
		P	U	P	C	J	C	P			J	C				
		L	S	H	A	C	S	I	K	C	A	H	T			
U	T	R	A	C	A	C	T	U	O	U	J	C	S	U		
S	U			J	L	O	L	Y	Q	M	A	C	K			
N	S			P	C	A	C	S	U	T	C	M	U	S	C	K
A	C			P	T	H	W	T	A	R	Y	V	T	Q	A	R
K	A			K	U	Z	C	T	U	K	P	L	C	Z	C	T
E	C	F	Q	K	L	S	C	A	C	T	U	S	C	A	J	A	U
V	T	S	C	O	R	P	I	O	N	H	I	G	K	C	T	W	S

Cactus Trail Challenge: Find the names of 3 animals that live in the desert.

1. _____   2. _____   3. _____

Name _____

In the Water

Which do you like better, swimming in a pool or swimming in a lake? _____

Why? _____

_____

Number the water activities from 1 to 9 to show how much you would like to do them. The one you want to do the most should be number 1.

_____ diving off the high dive

_____ jumping off the high dive

_____ going down a waterslide

_____ diving for things underwater

_____ swimming laps

_____ jumping off the low dive

_____ diving off the low dive

_____ racing a friend across the pool

_____ doing somersaults and headstands

Emma swims faster than Maria.
Maria swims slower than Amy.
Drew swims slower than Emma.

Write **T** if the statement is true, **F** if it is false, and **C** if you cannot tell.

_____ Maria is the slowest.

_____ Amy swims faster than Drew.

_____ Drew is the fastest.

_____ Emma swims faster than Drew and Amy.

_____ Emma and Amy swim at the same speed.

SIMILES

The water was as cold as _____.

The children splashed like _____.

The pool was as crowded as _____.

Name _____

In the Water

If you are going to swim in cold water, would you rather get used to it slowly or jump right in?

_____ Why? _____

_____

The word *pool* has double **O**s. Use the clues to find other words with double **O**s.

where you are now _____

liquid inside your body _____

using heat to prepare food _____

thief or criminal _____

a hammer or a screwdriver _____

animal in Australia _____

party decorations _____

popular team sport _____

where you sleep _____

Megan went to the beach 34 times last summer. She went 6 more times in July than she did in June. She went twice as many times in August as she did in June. How many times did Megan go to the beach during each month?

June: _____

July: _____

August: _____

Complete the sentences. Use at least 1 adjective or adverb in each of them.

_____ in the pool today.

_____ swam away _____

_____ in the lake?

In the Water

Ryan had a pool party for his birthday. For one of the games, Ryan's mother threw a bunch of coins into the pool so the children could dive for them. The chart below tells how much money and the number of coins that each child collected. Your job is to fill in how many of each kind of coin was collected. Use numbers or tallies to fill in the chart. **Hint:** It may help to use real coins.

Child	Amount	Number of Coins	Number of Coins Collected			
			Quarters	Dimes	Nickels	Pennies
Ryan	$0.81	7				
Amanda	$1.26	11				
Randy	$1.53	12				
Brooke	$0.97	8				
Simon	$2.32	15				
Syesha	$1.45	10				
Michael	$1.76	16				
Kristy	$0.85	11				
Jason	$1.01	12				
Paula	$1.29	15				
David	$2.53	20				
Carly	$2.00	22				

At the
Ice-Cream Store

What is the yummiest flavor of ice cream that you can think of? _____

What is the yuckiest flavor of ice cream that you can think of? _____

Karly is making a banana split. Number the steps from 1 to 10. The first step should be number 1.

_____ Scoop the ice cream.

_____ Add whipped cream.

_____ Cut the banana.

_____ Add sprinkles.

_____ Get a bowl.

_____ Eat it up!

_____ Put the banana in the bowl.

_____ Add chocolate sauce.

_____ Get a spoon.

_____ Peel the banana.

There are 2 kinds of cones: sugar and waffle. There are 3 flavors of ice cream: chocolate, vanilla, and strawberry. There are 3 toppings: sprinkles, nuts, and mini M&M's. How many different combinations of 1 cone, 1 scoop of ice cream, and 1 topping can you make?

_____ combinations

How many combinations would there be if there were 4 flavors of ice cream?

_____ combinations

The answer is **chocolate ice cream**. Write 3 different questions.

1. _____

2. _____

3. _____

Name _____

 # At the Ice-Cream Store

Write a sentence using the words *ice cream*, *paid*, *hot fudge*, and *baseball*.

_____

_____

Use the phone keypad to decode the ice-cream flavors. Remember, numbers 2 through 9 can represent one of 3 or 4 different letters. Example: *243779 = CHERRY*

8264552 _____

282253 486 _____

76259 7623 _____

7872923779 _____

246265283 2447 _____

Jim owns an ice-cream store. Use the clues to find out how many ice-cream cones he sold last week.

- He sold more than 300 but fewer than 350.

- The last digit is odd.

- The second digit is 3 less than the last digit.

- The sum of the first 2 digits equals the last digit.

- The sum of all the digits is 14.

Jim sold _____ **ice-cream cones.**

Everybody is talking about Jim's new ice-cream flavor, Triple Chocolate Dream. Each day, his sales for this flavor have tripled! How many scoops did Jim sell on each day?

Monday: 1 scoop

Tuesday: _____ scoops

Wednesday: _____ scoops

Thursday: _____ scoops

Friday: _____ scoops

Saturday: _____ scoops!

Name _____

At the Ice-Cream Store

Coach Clark took his team out for ice cream. Each player got a double-scoop cone and ordered a different combination of flavors than his teammates. There were 6 flavors of ice cream to choose from and 15 players on the team. Use the key to color the cones to show the 15 different combinations.

Chocolate ...... **Brown**
Strawberry... **Pink**
Blueberry ..... **Blue**
Lemon .... **Yellow**
Pistachio .... **Light Green**
Sherbet .... **Orange**

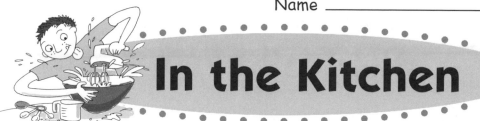

In the Kitchen

What are 5 things that you know how to make in the kitchen?

1. _____

2. _____

3. _____

4. _____

5. _____

8 ounces = 1 cup

16 tablespoons = 1 cup

How many ounces in $\frac{1}{4}$ cup? _____

How many tablespoons in $\frac{1}{4}$ cup? _____

How many ounces in $4\frac{1}{4}$ cups? _____

How many tablespoons in $6\frac{1}{2}$ cups? _____

This little story is full of homophones. Whenever you ~~sea won~~ see one, cross it off and ~~right~~ write the correct word above it.

The Knight Dad Maid Dinner

It was thyme four Dad two make dinner. First, he put the meetloaf in the oven. Then he pealed the potatoes and sliced the beats. The beats maid his cutting bored read. He put carats, celery, and tomatoes inn the salad. Their was pi four desert. Dinner was grate! After dinner, the hole family helped two clean up the kitchen. Dad said that he wood cook again next weak.

SIMILES

The fridge was as full as _____.

The pans clattered like _____.

The kitchen was as messy as _____.

Name _____

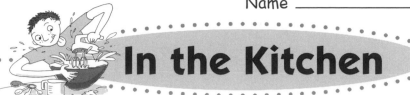

In the Kitchen

Write 2 things in your kitchen for each letter.

S_____ and S_____

P_____ and P_____

M_____ and M_____

R_____ and R_____

G_____ and G_____

T_____ and T_____

Circle the one in each pair that would be hardest to live without.

stove **or** refrigerator

forks **or** spoons

plates **or** bowls

dishwasher **or** microwave

chairs **or** tables

Complete the sentences.

_____ in the kitchen?

The refrigerator _____.

_____ the stove _____!

Add one more to each list.

mixing bowl, measuring cup, flour sifter, _____

spoon, fork, plate, _____

spatula, rubber scraper, wire whisk, _____

blender, crockpot, coffee maker, _____

sage, basil, cinnamon, _____

steamer, soup pot, teakettle, _____

Aubrey made 3 dozen cookies. Half have raisins. 30 have nuts. If no cookies are plain, how many have both raisins and nuts?

_____

Name _____

In the Kitchen

Use the clues to solve the crossword puzzle. The answers are things you would find in a kitchen.

ACROSS	DOWN
1. Get water here	**1.** For flipping pancakes
3. Make soup in this	**2.** Be careful! Don't cut yourself.
5. Use to get just the right amount of milk	**4.** Bake cookies in this
7. For serving punch or soup	**6.** Use to take the outside off
8. Eat cereal in this	**8.** Smoothie, please
12. Fill with juice	**9.** Ding! Food's ready!
13. In a shaker	**10.** Make an omelet in this
14. Eat soup with this	**11.** The burners are hot!
16. Where the milk is	**15.** Eating utensil with points
17. For browning bread	

Critical and Creative Thinking Activities • EMC 3395 • © Evan-Moor Corp.

At a Party

Write a sentence that is always true about parties.

_____

Write a sentence that is sometimes true about parties.

_____

Write a sentence that is never true about parties.

_____

Circle the letter of the statement that completes each syllogism.

All of the ice cream was chocolate.
All of the girls eat only vanilla ice cream.
Therefore, _____.

A. no girls ate chocolate ice cream

B. some girls ate chocolate ice cream

C. all girls ate cake

Some piñatas have clay pots inside.
All clay pots are easily broken.
Therefore, _____.

A. all piñatas are easily broken

B. some piñatas are easily broken

C. all clay pots are piñatas

Color the balloons with the correct colors.

• The red balloon is in front of the green and purple balloons but behind the blue balloon.

• The green balloon is in front of the yellow balloon but behind the blue balloon.

• The purple balloon is farthest to the right.

• The yellow balloon is farthest to the left.

At a Party

Add adjectives and adverbs to make the sentences more interesting.

The girl ate cake at the party.

_____

The piñata broke, and the children scrambled to get the candy.

_____

Use the clues to find things that might be at a party.

Pop!	B	_____
blow them out	C	_____
musical chairs	G	_____
full of candy	P	_____
don't let it melt	I	_____
open them	P	_____
for dancing	M	_____
on your head	H	_____

How many people came to the block party? Use the clues to find out.

• There were more than 50 people but fewer than 60.

• There were an odd number of kids and an odd number of adults.

• The tens digit is a higher number than the ones digit.

• The sum of the digits is 9.

_____ people

Explain a birthday party to someone who has never heard of one.

_____

_____

_____

_____

Name _____

At a Party

The names of the children who are going to the party are listed below. Fill in the missing letters on the party bags to make sure that each child gets a bag.

Barry	Cindy	Ginny	Jenny	Jimmy	Kenny	Sandy	Timmy
Kerry	Larry	Mandy	Mindy	Randy	Sammy	Tammy	Terry

___NNY

__A___Y

R____Y

M____Y

SA___Y

____RY

__IM___

TI_____

__I__Y

__AM__Y

T____Y

___N__Y

__IN___

___R__Y

M__N___

___N__Y

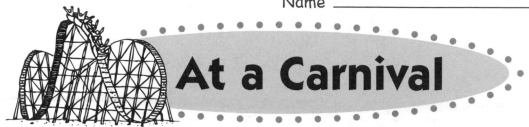

At a Carnival

Would you rather ride the Ferris wheel or the roller coaster? _____

Why? _____

Elly and Sharon bought tickets for the Ferris wheel, but they did <u>not</u> go on the ride. Give 3 possible reasons.

1. _____

2. _____

3. _____

Rides cost 2, 3, or 4 tickets. Rob had 25 tickets. He went on 9 rides and had one ticket left over. How many of each kind of ride did Rob go on?

2-ticket rides: _____

3-ticket rides: _____

4-ticket rides: _____

Circle 3 words that best describe your favorite kind of carnival ride.

slow	scary	spinning
dark	jerky	exciting
fast	high	unpredictable
loud	gentle	upside-down

Write an interrogatory sentence about the carnival.

_____

Write an exclamatory sentence about the carnival.

_____

Write a sentence about the carnival that contains quotation marks.

_____

At a Carnival

Name a food you can buy at the carnival that begins with each of the letters below.

H_____

S_____

C_____

P_____

I_____

F_____

What is your favorite carnival food?

_____

Jill, Kyle, Lauren, Miles, Nora, and Owen rode the roller coaster. Read the clues and write each child's name in the correct car.

• Two girls sat in the front car.

• Owen and Lauren did <u>not</u> sit in the middle car.

• Kyle sat behind a boy. No one sat behind Kyle.

• Jill did <u>not</u> sit in the same car as Lauren or Nora.

• Lauren and Miles each sat in the back seat of their cars.

Back

Front

The story below is full of spoonerisms (2-word phrases in which the first letters of the words are switched). When you see one, write the correct words above it.

Mike and Julie went to the carnival. First, they rode the ~~coller roaster~~.
                                                            roller coaster

Next, they got dot hogs and cow snones. After lunch, they went on the

cumper bars, and then Julie won a beddy tear by knocking down bilk mottles

with a bubber rall. When they were on the wherris Feel, they could see

Hike's mouse. Mike and Julie had a dice nay at the carnival.

At a Carnival

Each of the children below popped 5 balloons in the dart-throwing carnival game. Look at each score. Then circle the balloons that could have been popped.

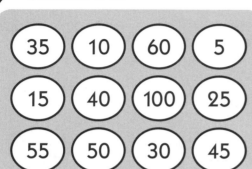

Jessica: 195

35	10	60	5
15	40	100	25
55	50	30	45

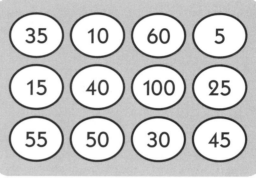

Keith: 200

35	10	60	5
15	40	100	25
55	50	30	45

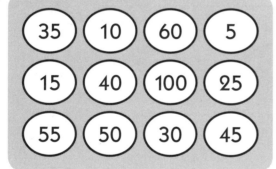

Lorenzo: 145

35	10	60	5
15	40	100	25
55	50	30	45

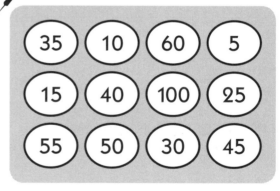

Jocelyn: 240

35	10	60	5
15	40	100	25
55	50	30	45

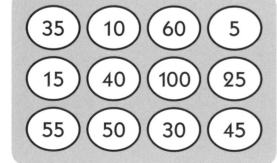

Carmen: 280

35	10	60	5
15	40	100	25
55	50	30	45

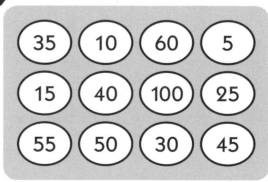

Scott: 105

35	10	60	5
15	40	100	25
55	50	30	45

At a Museum

Write a sentence that is always true about museums.

_____

Write a sentence that is sometimes true about museums.

_____

Write a sentence that is never true about museums.

_____

Andy's class went to a museum. They saw the paintings before the dinosaur exhibit. They saw the Egyptian exhibit after they saw the sculptures. They ate lunch before they saw the sculptures but after they saw the dinosaurs. Write the 5 activities in the correct order.

First: _____

Second: _____

Third: _____

Fourth: _____

Fifth: _____

Number the kinds of exhibits from 1 to 7 to show how much you would want to see them. The one you want to see the most should be number 1.

_____ Egyptian art and mummies

_____ Native American art

_____ paintings of landscapes

_____ an exhibit on World War II

_____ dinosaur bones

_____ sculptures of people

_____ optical illusions

Would you want to spend a night in a museum? _____

Why or why not? _____

_____

At a Museum

You are going to a museum. What are 3 things that would be good to know before you go?

1. _____

2. _____

3. _____

What was Kristina's favorite exhibit at the museum? Follow the directions and rewrite the word on each new line until you find out.

	K	R	I	S	T	I	N	A
Switch the 5th and the 6th letters.								
Make the 3rd letter the same as the 4th letter.								
Make the **T** into another letter that is made with 2 straight lines and that comes before **T** in the alphabet.								
Delete the 8th letter.								
Change the 1st letter to the 6th letter in the alphabet.								
Switch the 2nd and 7th letters.								
Change the **R** to the letter that comes after it in the alphabet.								
Change the **N** to the 4th vowel in the alphabet.								

Do you like going to a museum? _____

Why or why not? _____

_____

    Critical and Creative Thinking Activities • EMC 3395 • © Evan-Moor Corp.

Name _____

At a Museum

The children listed below all went to a museum on Saturday. They all arrived at different times and saw different exhibits first. Use the clues to find out who arrived when and what they each saw first. Make an **X** in a square when it cannot be an answer. Draw a circle when it is a correct answer. **Hint:** When you draw a circle in a square, you can make an **X** in all of the other squares in that row and column.

TODAY:
DINOSAURS
2:00 PM
MAIN AUDITORIUM

		Exhibits						Times Arrived					
		Dinosaurs	Mummies	African Art	Sculptures	Pioneer Days	Asian Art	9:00	9:30	10:00	10:30	11:00	11:30
Children	Max												
	Amber												
	Robert												
	Tonya												
	Vinnie												
	Kathy												

1. The girl who saw the Asian art first arrived at the museum at 10:30. The boy who saw the African art first arrived half an hour later.

2. The girl who saw the dinosaurs was the first to arrive at the museum. Vinnie arrived half an hour later. The boy who saw the mummies arrived next.

3. Tonya was the last to arrive. She did not see the Asian art or the dinosaurs.

4. Kathy did not see the dinosaurs or the sculptures first.

5. The person who arrived at 9:30 went to see the sculptures.

6. Max headed straight for the mummies. An hour later, he saw Robert, who had just arrived, in another exhibit.

At a Garage Sale

Do you like to buy things at garage sales? _____

Why or why not? _____

_____

Parker went to a garage sale that had books for sale. Paperbacks were $0.25 each and hardbacks were $0.50 each. Parker bought 17 books and paid $5.75. How many of each kind of book did Parker buy?

_____ paperbacks

_____ hardbacks

Jasmine's family is having a garage sale. She has decided to sell her stuffed animals. She has 7 big stuffed animals that she is planning to sell for $2.50 each and 13 small stuffed animals that she is planning to sell for $0.75 each. How much money will Jasmine make if she sells all of her stuffed animals?

$ _____

Use the clues to find the words.
The letters for each word can all be found in *GARAGE SALE*.

from a chicken _____

big _____

you have 2 _____

sea mammal _____

stare angrily _____

Make a sign for a garage sale that would catch people's attention.

At a Garage Sale

Your family is having a garage sale. List 5 items you would like to sell. Include the price you will charge for each item.

1. _____ $_____

2. _____ $_____

3. _____ $_____

4. _____ $_____

5. _____ $_____

Organize the garage sale items listed on the right so that each table will hold a different kind of item. Write the name of each item on the appropriate table. Then label the tables.

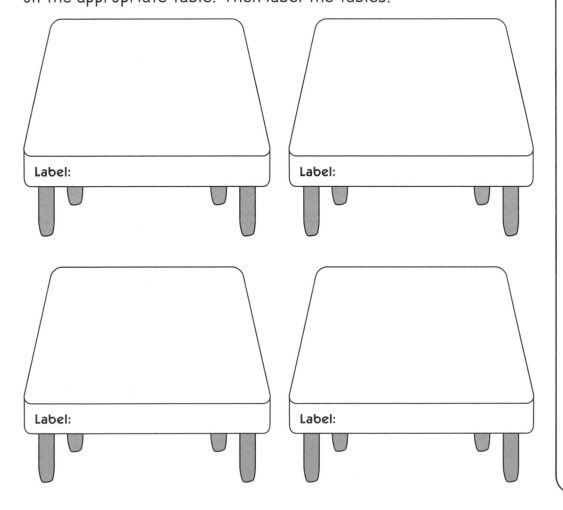

Label:

Label:

Label:

Label:

snow boots
jigsaw puzzle
T-shirt
coffee mug
fish tank
Monopoly game
jeans
dog leash
popcorn popper
belt
cat dish
casserole dish
in-line skates
baby booties
train set
cat toy
mixing bowl
sweater
teddy bear
spice rack
hamster cage
baseball cap
frying pan

At a Garage Sale

The 6 people listed below went to a garage sale. They all bought different items and paid different amounts. Use the clues to find out who bought which item and how much each customer paid. Make an **X** in a square when it <u>cannot</u> be an answer. Draw a circle when it is a correct answer. **Hint:** When you draw a circle in a square, you can make an **X** in all of the other squares in that row and column.

		Items Bought						Amounts Paid					
		Juice glasses	Popcorn popper	Chess set	Rain boots	Flower vase	Ski jacket	$1.00	$1.50	$2.00	$2.50	$3.00	$3.50
Customers	Nick												
	Sarah												
	Arnold												
	Talia												
	Bob												
	Tammy												

1. Arnold, Talia, and Bob all paid $2.50 or more for their items. None of them bought the flower vase.

2. None of the girls bought something to wear. None of the boys bought juice glasses or a popcorn popper.

3. The boy who bought the chess set used it to play chess with his sister, Tammy, who bought the flower vase.

4. Talia spent $1.00 more than Nick, who bought the rain boots.

5. Bob, who is an only child, paid more for his item than anyone else. Nick, who is also an only child, paid $1.50 less than Bob for his item.

6. Sarah paid 50¢ more for her item than Tammy paid for hers. Sarah does <u>not</u> know how to play chess.

7. The popcorn popper cost $1.50.

Name _____

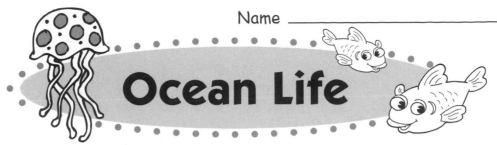

Ocean Life

If you were a fish or other animal that lives in the ocean, which one would you be?

_____ Why? _____

_____

What would be one disadvantage of being that animal? _____

_____

A large school of small fish was swimming in the ocean. A shark came along and ate $\frac{2}{3}$ of the fish. Then a group of seals ate half of the remaining fish. 7 of those fish were eaten by a larger fish. Of the fish that were left, $\frac{3}{4}$ got caught in a net. Now there are just 9 small fish. How many small fish were there to begin with?

_____ small fish

Draw It:

- There are 5 fish.
- The red fish is bigger than the blue fish.
- The green fish is smaller than the yellow fish.
- The blue fish is bigger than the yellow fish.
- The green fish is bigger than the orange fish.

How would you explain an octopus to someone who has never seen one?

_____

_____

_____

Name _____

Ocean Life

Finish the tongue twisters.

Willy Whale was _____

Sammy Seal saw _____

Four friendly fish _____

Circle the letter of the statement that completes each syllogism.

All sharks have fins.
All hammerheads are sharks.
Therefore, _____.

A. all sharks are hammerheads

B. some sharks have fins

C. all hammerheads have fins

All fish can swim.
No cats can swim.
Therefore, _____.

A. no cats are fish

B. all cats are fish

C. all cats can swim

Add adjectives and adverbs to make the sentence more interesting.

The shark chased the fish.

_____

SIMILES

The fish was as colorful as _____.

The whale was as big as _____.

The eel was as fast as _____.

The crab scampered across the sand like _____

_____

Ocean Life

Help each of the big fish below find dinner. Look at the number on the big fish. Then find the little fish with numbers that add up to that same number. Be sure to count the boxes first, because that's how many little fish you have to find. Write the numbers in the boxes. Each little fish can get eaten only once, and all of the little fish will be eaten. The first one is done for you.

Name _____

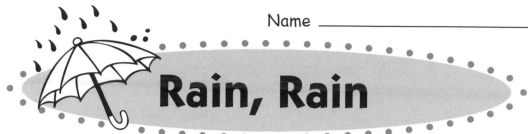

Rain, Rain

What does it mean when someone says it is "raining cats and dogs"? _____

_____

What are some other things it could be raining?

_____ and _____

_____ and _____

_____ and _____

_____ and _____

_____ and _____

Draw one of the things it could be raining.

Use the clues to find the words. Each word rhymes with *RAIN*.

cars on a track _____

spot on clothing _____

in the bathtub _____

country in Europe _____

connected rings _____

in your head _____

undecorated _____

It is raining and you do not want to get your hair wet. You don't have an umbrella, a hat, or a hood. What are 6 other things you could use?

1. _____

2. _____

3. _____

4. _____

5. _____

6. _____

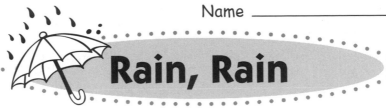

Rain, Rain

Complete each sentence.

The rain _____!

_____ your umbrella _____.

_____ rain boots?

Number the kinds of rain from 1 to 4. The lightest should be number 1 and the heaviest should be number 4.

_____ shower

_____ mist

_____ downpour

_____ drizzle

It rained more on Friday than it did on Sunday.
It rained less on Saturday than it did on Sunday.
It rained more on Monday than it did on Sunday.

Write **T** if the statement is true, **F** if it is false, and **C** if you cannot tell.

_____ More rain fell on Monday than on Saturday.

_____ More rain fell on Friday than on Monday.

_____ The least amount of rain fell on Saturday.

_____ It rained the same amount on Friday and Monday.

Circle the letter of the statement that completes each syllogism.

Red is a bright color.
Some umbrellas are red.
Therefore, _____.

A. all umbrellas are a bright color

B. some umbrellas are a bright color

C. all umbrellas are red

All plants need rain.
Some plants are trees.
Therefore, _____.

A. all trees need rain

B. some trees need rain

C. all plants are trees

Name _____

Rain, Rain

The chart below shows the rainfall for each month in Drizzletown for the past 2 years. Use the data to make a line graph on the grid. Then answer the questions. **Hint:** Write the months at the bottom and the numbers on the side. Use a different color for each year. Use the first letter of the word to label each month.

———— 2008
- - - - 2009

Month	2008	2009
Jan	7	6
Feb	6	5
Mar	4	6
Apr	5	6
May	3	5
Jun	2	1
Jul	1	2
Aug	1	1
Sep	2	3
Oct	3	6
Nov	10	8
Dec	6	7

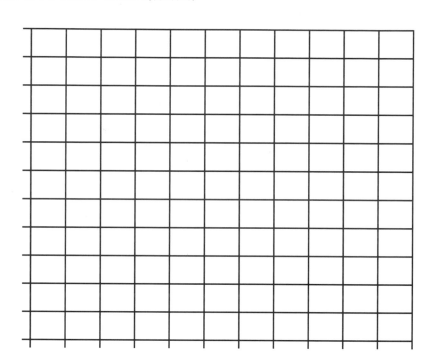

Did it rain more in March 2008 or March 2009? _____

What was the average monthly rainfall in 2009? _____

What are 3 statements you can make about the rain in Drizzletown in 2008 and 2009?

1. _____

2. _____

3. _____

Looking at your graph, which year do you think had the most rainfall? _____

Add to find each year's total. Were you correct? _____

Name _____

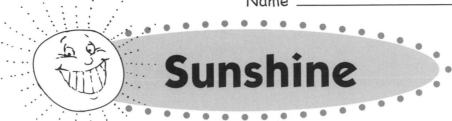

Sunshine

Without the sun, there could be no life on Earth. What are 5 different ways that people benefit from the sun?

1. _____

2. _____

3. _____

4. _____

5. _____

The sun is about 93 million miles from the Earth. If you went to the sun in a heatproof rocket that traveled at a rate of 5,000 miles per hour, how long would it take you to get there?

In hours: _____

In days: _____

About how many years is that?

_____

It was 6 degrees hotter on Friday than it was on Saturday. On Sunday, it was 11 degrees cooler than it was on Friday. On Saturday, it was 79 degrees. How hot was it on Friday and Sunday?

Friday: _____

Sunday: _____

SIMILES

The hot sand was like _____.

The sun was as bright as _____.

The girl's sunburn was as red as _____.

Name _____

Sunshine

What would happen to each one if you left it outside on a sunny day?

crayons: _____

a tuna fish sandwich: _____

a cup of water: _____

you: _____

Complete the *SUN* words.

before Monday	Sun_____
tall yellow plant	sun_____
end of the day	sun_____
ice-cream treat	sun_____
Ouch!	sun_____
eye protection	sun_____
shadow clock	sun_____

Make 3 different words by adding one letter to the word *SUN*.
Example: *STUN*

_____ _____ _____

The answer is **the sun**. Write 2 questions.

1. _____

2. _____

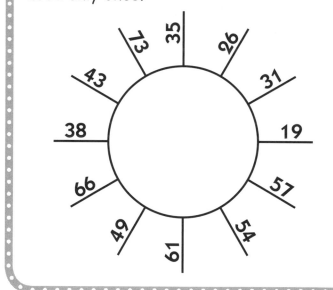

Draw lines across the sun to connect 2 rays that add up to **92**. You will draw 6 different lines, and each ray will be used only once.

73 35 26
43   31
38   19
66   57
49 61 54

Sunshine

Find the hidden joke and its answer. Read the directions below and cross off words. Then read the remaining words from left to right. Write the joke and its answer on the lines.

Joke

INDIGO	POWER	WHAT	HAPPY	TERRIFIC	TON
HAPPENED	SUNSHINE	CAT	TO	CAVES	PETS
BEAR	BEAUTIFUL	SOLAR	MAUVE	THE	QUART
MAN	IGLOO	WHO	PAPER	INTO	STAYED
MADE	SUPER	POT	UP	MAGENTA	QUACK
ALL	FADED	NIGHT	TERRIBLE	ADD	BIG
QUIVER	TEAL	PLAYFUL	SALAD	WONDERING	QUIZ
WHERE	HIDE	QUEEN	HOMEWORK	TAN	THE
ABSENT	AMBER	SUN	SPIT	POLAR	TINY
BORING	REED	BOAT	WENT	?	OUTSIDE

_____

_____

Answer

QUEST	IT	FILE	MAKEUP	FINALLY	KEYHOLE
TACKY	BEAST	DAWNED	BEIGE	WITHOUT	ON
SALES	POPCORN	HIDE	HIM	LOOP	QUIT

_____

- In each row, cross off the word that comes first in alphabetical order.
- Cross off each word with the pattern: **consonant, vowel, consonant, vowel, consonant.**
- Cross off the words that are 3 letters or longer and that make other words if you write them backward.
- Cross off the names of colors.
- Cross off the adjectives beginning with **B** or **T**.
- Cross off the words with **Q** in them.
- Cross off the compound words.

Snow Day!

Number the snow activities from 1 to 8 according to how much you would like to do them. The one you like the best should be number 1.

_____ building a snowman

_____ having a snowball fight

_____ sledding

_____ making snow angels

_____ taking a walk in the snow

_____ watching snow fall from indoors

_____ skiing or snowboarding

_____ building a snow fort

Marcos, Tanya, Alan, and Julia went sledding. The oldest child's sled was the fastest. The two youngest children went together on one sled. Tanya and Alan did <u>not</u> go together.

Write **T** if the statement is true, **F** if it is false, and **C** if you cannot tell.

_____ Julie and Marcos are the youngest.

_____ The oldest is Alan.

_____ Either Tanya or Alan went the fastest.

_____ Marcos is older than Julia.

_____ Tanya and Alan went together.

The answer is **a big snowball**. Write 3 different questions.

1. _____

2. _____

3. _____

SIMILES

The snow was as cold as _____.

The white snow was like _____.

The snowy path was as slippery as _____.

Snow Day!

If it snows three-fourths of an inch in half an hour, how many inches of snow will there be in 4 hours?

_____ inches

In 7½ hours?

_____ inches

What are 5 things besides a carrot that would make a good nose for a snowman?

1. _____

2. _____

3. _____

4. _____

5. _____

You want to go out and play in the snow, but you cannot find a pair of mittens or gloves. What do you do?

_____

People often put sand on the road to keep their cars from slipping on the ice and snow. Explain why this works.

_____

_____

Draw It:
There are 3 snowmen. The one on the right is the tallest. The one in the middle is the shortest. The tallest snowman is holding a shovel. The snowman on the left is the only one <u>not</u> wearing a hat. The shortest snowman is wearing a scarf. All of the snowmen are smiling.

Name _____

Snow Day!

Pretend that you are looking down on a long patch of snow from above. For each situation, draw what the prints would look like going from one end to the other.

an adult and a child walking side by side

a person and a dog

a person dragging a stick

a person pulling a sled with runners

Critical and Creative Thinking Activities • EMC 3395 • © Evan-Moor Corp.

Earthquakes and Volcanoes

Which would be scarier, to be caught near a volcano when it erupts or to be caught in a big earthquake?

_____ Why? _____

_____

Use the clues to find the words. The letters can all be found in *VOLCANOES*.

helps to walk _____

not to win _____

nearby _____

chilly _____

caverns _____

not crazy _____

on your face _____

not tight _____

paddle in them _____

Scientists estimate that about 500,000 earthquakes occur each year on our planet. Most of these cannot be felt and very few cause damage. If there are 500,000 earthquakes in a year, about how many occur each day? Circle the correct answer.

A. more than 2,000

B. more than 1,000

C. less than 1,000

D. less than 500

Complete each sentence.

The earthquake _____!

_____ the volcano _____?

Earthquakes and Volcanoes

Write a sentence that is always true about earthquakes.

_____

Write a sentence that is sometimes true about earthquakes.

_____

Write a sentence that is never true about earthquakes.

_____

During the earthquake, the books fell off the shelf before the flower vase broke. The flower vase broke after the window cracked. The sugar spilled before the books fell off the shelf.

Write **T** if the statement is true, **F** if it is false, and **C** if you cannot tell.

_____ The sugar spilled first.

_____ The books fell before the window cracked.

_____ The sugar spilled after the books fell.

_____ The flower vase broke after the books fell.

_____ No one really liked the flower vase anyway.

Read the directions below and cross off letters in the grid to find the name of a volcano that erupted in Washington state on May 18, 1980.

E	M	O	D	H	U	J	N	T
S	W	A	I	M	E	N	E	T
X	H	V	E	L	I	E	N	S

• In the first row, cross off the letters that come before **L** in the alphabet.

• In the second row, cross off the letters that are made with 4 lines.

• In the third row, cross off the letters that represent 1, 5, and 10 in Roman numerals.

The volcano that erupted is:

_____

Earthquakes and Volcanoes

Read the directions below and cross off words to reveal 3 interesting facts about Mount Saint Helens. Write the facts on the lines.

FACT 1

THE	DAY	ERUPTION	VERY	264	SENT
DEER	OVER	WENT	540	SADLY	MILLION
DIRTY	TONS	BEARS	OF	245	UNDER
VOLCANIC	WONDER	ASH	QUICKLY	INTO	683
THROUGH	THE	174	AIR	SERIOUSLY	RABBITS

_____

_____

FACT 2

THE	VIOLENTLY	200	VIOLIN	MILE	MICE
BIRDS	AN	LAST	192	HOUR	HARDLY
BLAST	534	SMOKE	OF	BADLY	FIRE
SQUIRRELS	AND	ASH	SQUIRT	DESTROYED	150
SQUARE	WIVES	MILES	OF	480	FOREST

_____

_____

FACT 3

SCIENTISTS	822	SILENCE	EXPECT	FROGS	336
PORCUPINES	MOUNT	RACCOONS	SAINT	SAME	HELENS
TO	605	HAVE	TRUE	ANOTHER	BIG
ERUPTION	IN	THROW	THE	SKUNKS	NEXT
50	YELLOW	TO	100	YEARS	FISH

_____

_____

- Cross off the word in each row that would come last in alphabetical order.
- Cross off the names of animals.
- Cross off the numbers with digits that add up to 12.
- Cross off the odd numbers.
- Cross off the words that end in **y**.

Name _____

Giant Squid

Giant squid are really big. The largest squid ever found was nearly 60 feet long! If you put squid that size end to end on a football field, how many would it take to reach from one end to the other?
Hint: A football field is 360 feet long.

_____ giant squid

Most squid are not quite 60 feet long. How many squid would it take to reach from one end of a football field to the other if the squid were 40 feet long?

_____ giant squid

A giant squid has 8 arms and 2 tentacles. How many arms and tentacles do 97 giant squid have?

_____ squid arms

_____ squid tentacles

How about 178 giant squid?

_____ squid arms

_____ squid tentacles

Giant squid are rarely seen by people. Why do you think that is?

_____

A giant squid sees a school of small fish. Instead of making some of the fish her lunch, she swims away. Give 3 possible reasons.

1. _____

2. _____

3. _____

     Critical and Creative Thinking Activities • EMC 3395 • © Evan-Moor Corp.

Giant Squid

Write 3 facts about giant squid.

1. _____

2. _____

3. _____

Write 3 opinions about giant squid.

1. _____

2. _____

3. _____

The word *squid* contains the letters *qu*. Use the clues to find other *qu* words.

4-sided shape _____

2 pints _____

fast _____

short test _____

to stop early _____

she who rules _____

duck sound _____

Shh! _____

for arrows _____

vegetable _____

A squid has 8 arms. Use **+**, **−**, **×**, and **÷** to make 8 equations that all have an answer of **8**.

$$12 \quad 15 \quad 19 = 8$$

$$3 \quad 4 \quad 4 = 8$$

$$4 \quad 6 \quad 3 = 8$$

$$9 \quad 5 \quad 2 = 8$$

$$21 \quad 7 \quad 4 \quad 1 = 8$$

$$6 \quad 3 \quad 2 \quad 12 = 8$$

$$9 \quad 2 \quad 2 \quad 6 = 8$$

$$5 \quad 4 \quad 10 \quad 2 = 8$$

Name _____

Giant Squid

Each arm on this giant squid has suction cups containing numbers that make a pattern. Fill in the missing numbers to complete the number pattern on each arm.

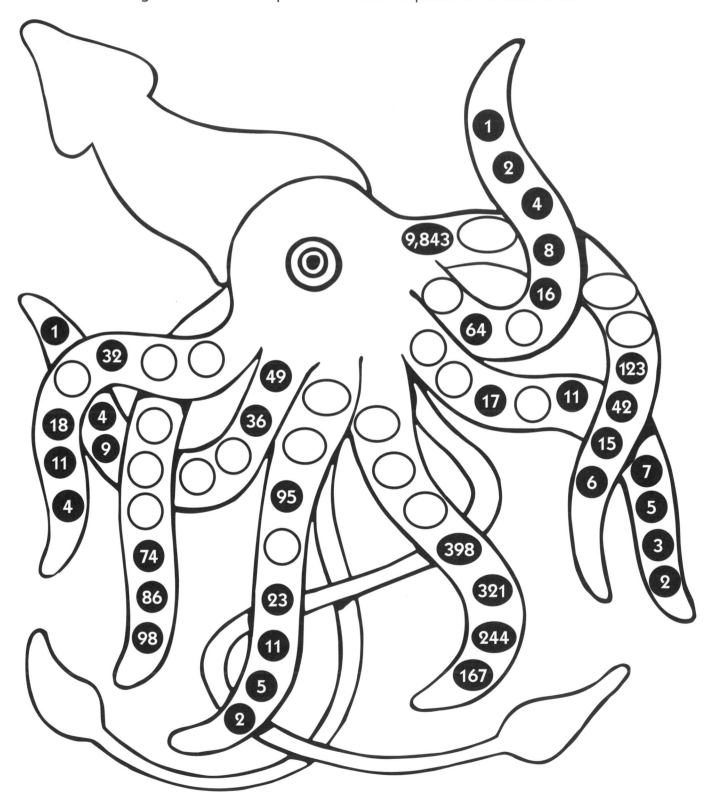

Critical and Creative Thinking Activities • EMC 3395 • © Evan-Moor Corp.

Name _____

Bears

Write a sentence using the homophones *bear* and *bare*.

_____

Write a sentence about a grizzly bear. Use exactly 11 words.

_____

Start with the word *BEAR*. Change only one letter to make a new word. Then change one letter in the new word to make another word. Try to fill all 10 lines with 10 different words.

BEAR

1. _____

2. _____

3. _____

4. _____

5. _____

6. _____

7. _____

8. _____

9. _____

10. _____

Ginny likes to collect teddy bears. She has three-and-a-half times as many brown bears as black bears. She has twice as many black bears as white bears. Ginny has 4 white teddy bears. Fill in the number of teddy bears that Ginny has.

Black teddy bears: _____

Brown teddy bears: _____

All teddy bears: _____

Name Ginny's 4 white teddy bears. Each name must have something to do with the color **white**.

1. _____

2. _____

3. _____

4. _____

Name _____

Bears

What if people hibernated like bears do? Fill in the chart with 3 advantages and 3 disadvantages.

Advantages	Disadvantages

How many different kinds of bears can you name?

1. _____   3. _____   5. _____

2. _____   4. _____   6. _____

Bob the Bear had an exciting day! He ate some berries after he scratched his back on a tree trunk. He wandered around the woods before he took a drink from the stream. He scratched his back on the tree after he drank from the stream. Write the 4 things Bob did in the correct order.

First: _____

Second: _____

Third: _____

Fourth: _____

Bears are omnivores and will eat almost anything. What are 6 things that you think bears eat in the wild?

1. _____

2. _____

3. _____

4. _____

5. _____

6. _____

Critical and Creative Thinking Activities • EMC 3395 • © Evan-Moor Corp.

Bears

Use the clues to fill in the horizontal boxes. When you are done, the vertical boxes outlined in bold will spell out the name of a constellation that looks like a bear.

1. What baby bears are called

2. Large brown bear

3. A bear's strongest sense

4. Smokey Bear is this type

5. What the bear went "over" in a song

6. Bears like to eat this large, pink-fleshed fish

7. Park where Yogi Bear lives

8. White bear

9. What bears do in winter

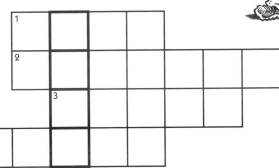

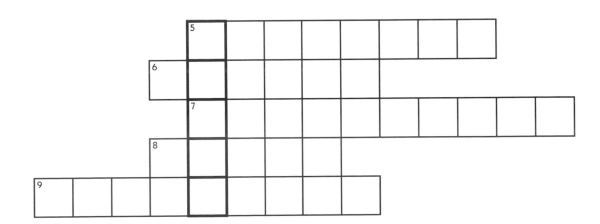

The name of a constellation that looks like a bear is _____.

Name _____

Dinosaurs

Which would be more challenging to keep as a pet, a Tyrannosaurus or a Brontosaurus?

_____ Why? _____

_____

When people make models of dinosaurs, they must guess about skin color since no one really knows. What color skin do you think the Tyrannosaurus had?

_____ Why do you think so? _____

_____

One of the biggest dinosaurs was the Seismosaurus. This giant measured about 145 feet from head to tail. If you had a bunch of kids about the same size as you are, about how many would you have to line up head to foot for the line to be as long as a Seismosaurus?

_____ kids

There are 5,280 feet in a mile. If you lined up a bunch of Seismosauruses head to tail, about how many would you need to make a mile?

_____ Seismosauruses

SIMILES

The Brachiosaurus was as big as _____.

The Velociraptor was as vicious as _____.

The teeth of the Tyrannosaurus were like _____.

Name _____

Dinosaurs

There are many theories about why the dinosaurs became extinct. Make up a silly theory about this mystery.

The dinosaurs became extinct because _____

_____

_____

_____.

Fill in the Venn diagram with at least 3 things in each section.

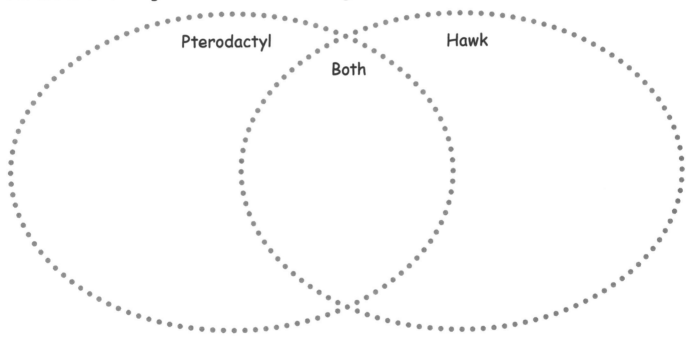

Pterodactyl   Hawk

Both

Oh dear, you have accidentally entered a time portal which has sent you back to the time of the dinosaurs! Not only that, a large meat-eating dinosaur has just spotted you. What are 3 things that you can do to keep from being eaten?

1. _____

2. _____

3. _____

Dinosaurs

Dinosaurs are often given Greek or Latin names that describe them. For example, the name "Brontosaurus" means *thunder* (bronto) *lizard* (saurus). Use the chart to find what these other dinosaur names mean.

Allosaurus _____

Velociraptor _____

Deinonychus _____

Diceratops _____

Monolophosaurus _____

Ornithomimus _____

Micropachycephalosaurus _____

_____

Write a dinosaur name for each description.

sharp claw _____

flat head lizard _____

winged thief _____

pointed-tailed lizard _____

thick-skinned lizard _____

big-toothed lizard _____

Make up a dinosaur of your own. Draw a picture of it on the back, and then name it.

allo	strange
alti	tall
angusti	sharp
apato	deceptive
canthus	spiked
cephalo	head
cera	horned
cyclo	round
deino	terrible
denti	tooth
derm	skin
di	two
lopho	ridged
luro	tail
macro	large
mega	large
micro	small
mimus	mimic
mono	single
mucro	pointed
nychus	claw
ornitho	bird
pachy	thick
ped	foot
placo	flat
poly	many
ptero	winged
raptor	thief
saurus	lizard
tops	head
tri	three
veloci	fast

Critical and Creative Thinking Activities • EMC 3395 • © Evan-Moor Corp.

Name _____

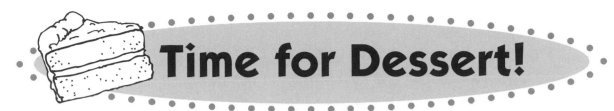

Time for Dessert!

About how many desserts a week do you think a person your age should eat? _____

Why? _____

Do you think you will eat more or fewer desserts when you are an adult? _____

Why? _____

Rate the desserts from 1 to 10 according to how much you like them. The one you like the most should be number 1.

_____ hot fudge sundae

_____ apple pie

_____ orange jello

_____ chocolate cake

_____ carrot cake

_____ vanilla pudding

_____ chocolate chip cookies

_____ lemon bars

_____ brownies

_____ strawberry shortcake

Use the list of desserts that you rated to answer the questions below.

Would you rather have the dessert you rated number **5** every day for the next year or have the dessert you rated number **1** once a week for the next year?

_____

Which dessert would your mother choose as her favorite?

_____

How about your father?

_____

Which dessert do you think would be the hardest to make?

_____

Write a sentence about dessert. Use exactly 5 words.

_____

Time for Dessert!

Carrie's father has made her favorite dessert, but Carrie does not eat any of it. List 3 possible reasons.

1. _____

2. _____

3. _____

Name a dessert that...

is creamy _____

is gooey _____

is crunchy _____

contains cinnamon _____

has nuts in it _____

smells good _____

you do <u>not</u> like _____

Cody has made brownies in a large rectangular pan. He wants to cut the batch into exactly 24 brownies. How many cuts will he need to make?

_____ cuts

Think of a dessert. Write sentences to tell about it.

Write a sentence that is always true about the dessert.

_____

Write a sentence that is sometimes true about the dessert.

_____

Write a sentence that is never true about the dessert.

_____

Time for Dessert!

The Miller family went out for dinner. Each member of the family ordered a different dessert at a different price. Use the clues to find out who ordered each dessert and what each dessert cost. Make an **X** in a square when it <u>cannot</u> be an answer. Draw a circle when it is a correct answer. **Hint:** When you draw a circle in a square, you can make an **X** in all of the other squares in that row and column.

		Desserts						Prices					
		Chocolate cake	Apple pie	Berry torte	Ginger cookies	Ice cream	Lemon pudding	$3.00	$3.25	$3.50	$3.75	$4.00	$4.25
Family Members	Caitlyn												
	Blake												
	Mom												
	Dad												
	Grandma												
	Grandpa												

1. The man who ordered ginger cookies gave one to his son, who likes lemon pudding.

2. The female who had the berry torte ordered the most expensive dessert.

3. The lemon pudding was the least expensive dessert. Grandma's dessert cost a dollar more than the lemon pudding.

4. Grandma and Grandpa do <u>not</u> eat chocolate. Grandma <u>cannot</u> eat dairy.

5. Mom did <u>not</u> order anything with fruit in it. Her dessert cost 50¢ more than Blake's.

6. The dessert that Dad ordered cost half a dollar more than the one that Grandpa got.

Pizza

Explain a pizza to someone who has never seen or tasted one.

_____

_____

_____

What is Lorenzo's favorite pizza topping? Follow the directions and rewrite the word on each new line until you find out.

	L	O	R	E	N	Z	O
Change the fourth letter to the letter that comes just before **T** in the alphabet.							
Change the first **O** to the vowel that is in both *LAUGHTER* and *SAILING*.							
Change the second **O** to the vowel that is in both *EATING* and *CUTE*.							
Make the fifth letter the same as the second letter.							
Change the first letter to the letter that is used most often to make a singular word plural.							
Change the second-to-the-last letter to the seventh letter in the alphabet.							
Change the third letter to the letter that comes three letters after it in the alphabet.							

What is your favorite pizza topping? _____

The answer is **a pepperoni pizza**. Write 3 different questions.

1. _____

2. _____

3. _____

Name _____

Pizza

Mr. Jacobs and Ms. Allan are giving their 5th-grade classes a pizza party. There are 27 students in Mr. Jacobs' class and 26 students in Ms. Allan's class. The teachers would like each student to get 2 slices of pizza. Each pizza is divided into 16 slices. How many pizzas should they order?

_____ pizzas

How many slices will be left over?

_____ slices

The Olson family is going out for pizza. They are trying to decide which is the better deal: a large pizza or the all-you-can-eat special. A large pizza costs $17.50. For the all-you-can-eat special, Mom and Dad would cost $5.50 each and their kids, Jake and Jim, would cost $3.75 each. Which deal is less expensive?

_____

Write a sentence using the words *pizza*, *cheese*, *slice*, and *saxophone*.

_____

_____

9 people are sharing these 2 pizzas. Divide the pizzas into equal slices so that everyone gets the same amount.

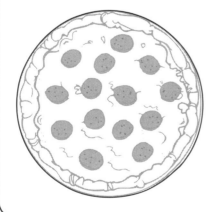 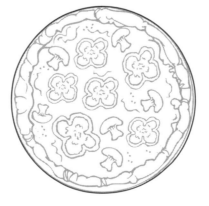

The word *pizza* has double consonants. Can you think of 5 other foods with double consonants?

1. _____

2. _____

3. _____

4. _____

5. _____

Pizza

3 pizzas have been ordered for the team pizza party. Each pizza has 10 slices. Each of the 15 players gets 2 slices of pizza. Your job is to make sure that each player gets 2 slices of pizza that he or she likes. You may give a player 2 slices of the same pizza or of 2 different pizzas. Use numbers to show what kind of pizza the players will get. When you are done, every slice should be assigned to a player.

Pizza 1	**Pizza 2**	**Pizza 3**
	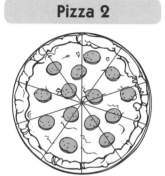	
Veggie Delight	Pepperoni	Ham and Pineapple

Cassie will eat anything. _____ and _____	**Lila** is allergic to pepperoni. _____ and _____	**Jarid** is allergic to pineapple. _____ and _____
Kelly wants a lot of meat. _____ and _____	**Amber** does not like pepperoni. _____ and _____	**Olivia** likes pineapple and pepperoni. _____ and _____
Joshua loves pepperoni. _____ and _____	**Marcus** loves pepperoni. _____ and _____	**Chandra** likes ham but not pepperoni. _____ and _____
Micah does not eat ham. _____ and _____	**Solomon** does not like pepperoni. _____ and _____	**Benjamin** wants ham and pineapple. _____ and _____
Lucy loves vegetables. _____ and _____	**David** is a vegetarian. _____ and _____	**Tina** does not like vegetables. _____ and _____

SSSlurp!

Start with the word *SOUP*. Change only one letter to make a new word. Then change one letter in the new word to make another word. Can you fill all 10 lines, changing only one letter each time?

SOUP

1. _____

2. _____

3. _____

4. _____

5. _____

6. _____

7. _____

8. _____

9. _____

10. _____

Jody eats 3 bowls of soup each week. How many bowls of soup will she eat in a year?

_____ bowls of soup

Unscramble the names of things you might find in soup. Then find them in the word search.

SNEBA _____

CRIE _____

ROSTRAC _____

LABRYE _____

NORC _____

STELLIN _____

TOASTOPE _____

KINCEHC _____

DOESNOL _____

MOEATTSO _____

N	S	B	E	A	N	S	N	T
N	L	T	P	Y	G	B	E	O
O	I	N	O	O	P	S	K	M
O	T	A	T	R	B	K	C	A
D	N	Z	A	U	R	J	I	T
L	E	V	T	B	O	A	H	O
E	L	W	O	K	R	I	C	E
S	X	Y	E	L	R	A	B	S
P	T	J	S	K	C	O	R	N

SSSlurp!

How many different kinds of soup can you name?

1. _____ 4. _____ 7. _____

2. _____ 5. _____ 8. _____

3. _____ 6. _____ 9. _____

Circle the letter of the correct statement to complete each syllogism.

All carrots are vegetables.

Some soups have carrots.

Therefore, _____.

A. all soups have vegetables

B. some soups have vegetables

C. all vegetables are carrots

Everything homemade is yummy.

Some soups are homemade.

Therefore, _____.

A. some soups are yummy

B. all soups are yummy

C. some soups are salads

Here is a bowl of alphabet soup. How many words can you make using 4 or more letters? Use the back if you need to.

1. _____ 9. _____

2. _____ 10. _____

3. _____ 11. _____

4. _____ 12. _____

5. _____ 13. _____

6. _____ 14. _____

7. _____ 15. _____

8. _____ 16. _____

  Critical and Creative Thinking Activities • EMC 3395 • © Evan-Moor Corp.

Name _____

SSSlurp!

It's time to make soup, but you have a double challenge. You must decide what to put in the soup to make it yummy, and you must also make sure that the points are correct. Good luck and happy cooking!

Ingredient	Points
Carrots	5 each
Celery	6 each
Onions	7 each
Potatoes	8 each
Corn	9 per cup
Lentils	10 per cup
Black beans	11 per cup
Noodles	12 per cup
Barley	13 per cup
Rice	14 per cup
Chicken	20
Beef	30
Spices	50

Make a soup that is between 100 and 120 points.

Ingredient	Amount	Points
Total Points:		

Make a soup that is between 125 and 150 points.

Ingredient	Amount	Points
Total Points:		

Make a soup that is between 155 and 200 points.

Ingredient	Amount	Points
Total Points:		

Name _____

School Lunch

Rate your school's hot lunch program.

yummy	1..........2..........3..........4..........5	yucky
varied menu	1..........2..........3..........4..........5	same old stuff
nutritious	1..........2..........3..........4..........5	unhealthy
inexpensive	1..........2..........3..........4..........5	expensive

School lunch costs $2.35 at Sharon's school. Sharon bought lunch 58 times during the school year. How much did Sharon spend on school lunch?

$ _____

Tony goes to the same school as Sharon. His mother gave him a lot of change to pay for lunch today—21 coins! How many of each coin does Tony have?

_____ quarters   _____ dimes

_____ nickels   _____ pennies

Create the worst school lunch that you can imagine.
Draw it on the tray, and then label each item.

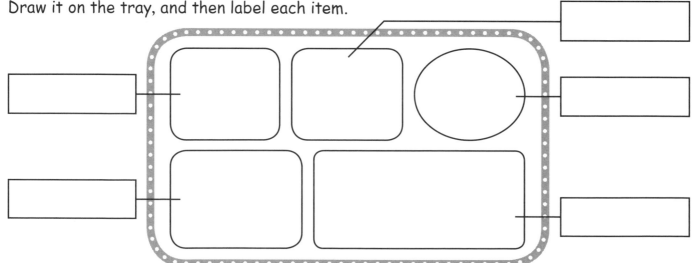

Name _____

School Lunch

Do you like buying school lunch? _____

Why or why not? _____

Today, there are two main-dish choices for hot lunch: pizza and a sub sandwich. For fruit, students may choose an apple or an orange. For dessert, there is a cookie or a cupcake. For a beverage, there is chocolate milk or plain milk. How many different combinations of main dish, fruit, dessert, and beverage are there?

_____ different combinations

Which would you choose for each one?

Main dish: _____

Fruit: _____

Dessert: _____

Beverage: _____

Many kids who pack their lunches bring sandwiches. How many different kinds of sandwiches can you name?

1. _____

2. _____

3. _____

4. _____

5. _____

6. _____

7. _____

8. _____

9. _____

10. _____

Draw a ★ next to the one you like the most. Make an X next to the ones you do not like.

SIMILES

The meatball was as hard as _____.

The pizza was as greasy as _____.

The rubbery meat was like _____.

School Lunch

All of the children listed below are very picky about the lunches they eat at school. Each of the items in each child's lunch must start with the same letter as his or her name. Fill in the chart to make each child a lunch.

Name	Main Dish	Fruit or Veggie	Snack or Dessert	Drink
Sarah				
Pete				
Carlos				
Trina				
Michael				
Fiona				
Gina				

Garrett and Jennifer both have double letters in their names. Can you make two different lunches that both have foods with double letters?

Name	Main Dish	Fruit or Veggie	Snack or Dessert	Drink
Garrett				
Jennifer				

Breakfast

What do you usually eat for breakfast? _____

If you could have anything you wanted for breakfast tomorrow morning, what would you choose?

_____

_____

Jenna eats a bowl of cereal each and every morning. There are 12 servings in a box of cereal. About how many boxes of cereal will Jenna eat in a year? Round to a whole number.

_____ boxes

A box of cereal costs $4.75. About how much will a year's supply of Jenna's cereal cost?

$_____

Jenna's brother also eats this cereal. If he eats 2 bowls a day, how much will it cost for both children for a year?

$_____

Write a sentence that is always true about breakfast.

_____

Write a sentence that is sometimes true about breakfast.

_____

Write a sentence that is never true about breakfast.

_____

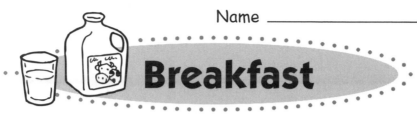

Name _____

Breakfast

Many people believe that breakfast is the most important meal of the day. Why do you think this is?

_____

_____

Kit has made a yummy bowl of oatmeal. She added milk to her oatmeal before she added raisins. She added almonds after the milk. She added brown sugar before the raisins.

Write **T** if the statement is true, **F** if it is false, and **C** if you cannot tell.

_____ Kit added raisins after the milk.

_____ Kit added almonds before the brown sugar.

_____ Kit added milk before the brown sugar.

_____ Kit added raisins and almonds at the same time.

_____ Kit added raisins after the brown sugar.

_____ Kit likes oatmeal.

How many different breakfast foods can you think of?

1. _____

2. _____

3. _____

4. _____

5. _____

6. _____

7. _____

8. _____

9. _____

10. _____

Complete the sentences.

_____ pancakes and maple syrup _____.

_____ for breakfast?

Eggs are not _____.

Name _____

Breakfast

Solve the breakfast crossword puzzle ... don't eat it!

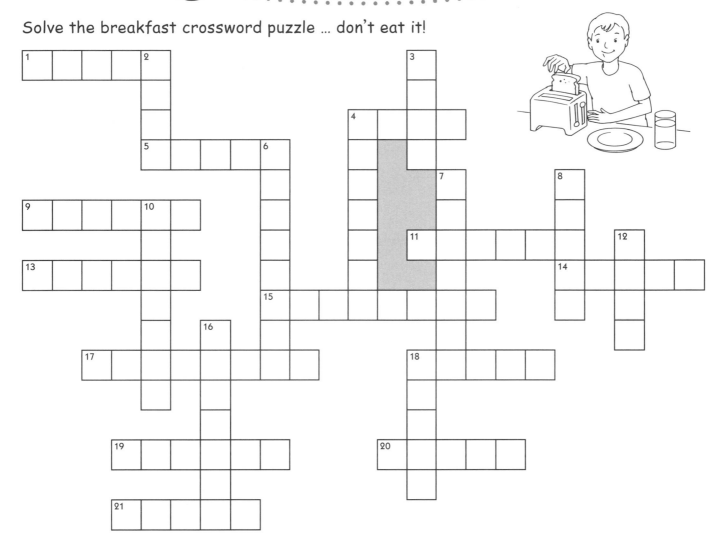

ACROSS

1. Breakfast drink
4. Good on cereal
5. Good on pancakes
9. Plain or fruit-flavored milk product
11. Fruit with a yellow peel
13. Blueberry or bran
14. Use to eat cereal
15. Glazed with a hole
17. In a stack with syrup
18. Breakfast meat in strips
19. Breakfast food in a box
20. Fruit spread
21. Kind of syrup

DOWN

2. Scramble or fry them
3. Yellow part of an egg
4. Breakfast time
6. 3 bears' food
7. For flipping pancakes
8. Heated bread
10. Dried grapes
12. Holds your oatmeal
16. A cooked cereal
18. Good with cream cheese

Name _____

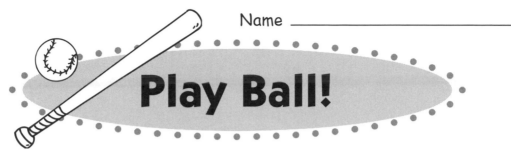

Play Ball!

Write 3 ways that the game of baseball would change if the ball were cube-shaped.

1. _____

2. _____

3. _____

Write 3 ways that the game of baseball would change if it were played in a swamp.

1. _____

2. _____

3. _____

SIMILES

The pitch was as fast as _____.

The crack of the bat was like _____.

The cheering of the crowd was like _____.

How are basketball and baseball the same and different? Write 3 ways for each.

Same	Different

Name _____

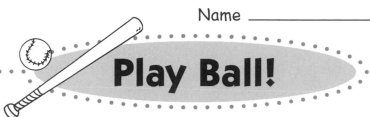

Play Ball!

Would you rather be the best player on a losing team or the worst player on a winning team?

_____ Why? _____

_____

Would you rather play all your games in perfect weather but lose all of them, or would you rather win every game but always have to play in the rain?

_____ Why? _____

_____

"It's not whether you win or lose, it's how you play the game."

Do you agree with this saying? _____

Why or why not? _____

Amber, Carly, Rachel, and Zoe all play on the same softball team. Read the clues to find out who plays each position.

- Zoe is not the pitcher or the shortstop.

- Rachel, who is not the catcher, did not throw the ball to Carly or Zoe when she helped to get a batter out at first base.

- Carly is best friends with the shortstop.

First base: _____

Pitcher: _____

Catcher: _____

Shortstop: _____

Write a sentence using the words *baseball*, *bat*, *hit*, and *hippopotamus*.

_____

Name _____

Play Ball!

Think of sports or games that use a ball, and then write them on the lines.
Follow the directions below to fill in the boxes.

1. _____ ☐   7. _____ ☐

2. _____ ☐   8. _____ ☐

3. _____ ☐   9. _____ ☐

4. _____ ☐   10. _____ ☐

5. _____ ☐   11. _____ ☐

6. _____ ☐   12. _____ ☐

First, read the directions and fill in the boxes above. Then write the names of the
sports where they belong in the Venn diagram.

• Write **T** in the box if it's a team sport.

• Write **H** in the box if the sport
  involves hitting the ball
  with something.

• Draw a ★ in the box if it's
  one of your **favorite** sports.

Favorites

Team

Hit

It's All About Speed

In some sports, it is important to be able to go fast. Name as many of those sports as you can.

1. _____   4. _____   7. _____

2. _____   5. _____   8. _____

3. _____   6. _____   9. _____

Circle the letter of the statement that completes each syllogism.

Some people are runners.
All runners are fast.
Therefore, _____.

A. some runners are people

B. some people are fast

C. all people are fast

Some women like pizza.
Some skiers are women.
Therefore, _____.

A. all skiers like pizza

B. no skiers like pizza

C. some skiers like pizza

Read the statements below, and then fill in the chart to show the miles each person can run in the number of minutes shown. Reduce the fractions.

• Janet can run a mile in 6 minutes.

• Jack can run a mile in 8 minutes.

• Chrissy can run a mile in 10 minutes.

Minutes	Janet	Jack	Chrissy
4 minutes			
12 minutes			
18 minutes			
20 minutes			
24 minutes			

Name _____

It's All About Speed

Which of these kinds of races would you most like to be in: ski, horse, or bike?

_____ Why? _____

Which of those kinds of races do you think is the most dangerous? _____

Why? _____

Besides a car, what is the fastest thing you have ever ridden on or in? _____

Number the activities from 1 to 4 according to how fast you can do them. The one you can do the fastest should be number 1. _____ skating _____ swimming _____ running _____ biking	Four girls had a race. Blair was faster than Natalie. Natalie was faster than Jo. Jo was slower than Blair. Tootie was faster than Blair. In what order did the girls finish the race? First: _____ Second: _____ Third: _____ Fourth: _____

What does it mean to "jump the gun" in a race?

_____

What does it mean to "jump the gun" in a situation that is <u>not</u> a race?

_____

Use the expression "jump the gun" in a sentence.

_____

Critical and Creative Thinking Activities • EMC 3395 • © Evan-Moor Corp.

Name _____

It's All About Speed

The 5 children listed below all ride their bikes to school. Fill in the chart to show each child's average speed. Then use the chart to answer the questions.
Hint: *mph* means *miles per hour.*

	Monday	Tuesday	Wednesday	Thursday	Friday	Average
Chris	11 mph	12 mph	14 mph	16 mph	12 mph	
Tracy	11 mph	10 mph	13 mph	14 mph	12 mph	
Danny	15 mph	13 mph	16 mph	17 mph	14 mph	
Laurie	17 mph	15 mph	16 mph	19 mph	18 mph	
Keith	19 mph	17 mph	18 mph	17 mph	19 mph	

Which child had the fastest speed on Thursday?   _____

Which child had the fastest speed on Monday?   _____

Which child had the fastest average speed?   _____

What is the average speed of all 5 children?   _____

The school is 4 miles from Danny's house.
How long did it take him to get to school on Wednesday?   _____ minutes

Keith lives 3 miles from the school.
How long did it take him to ride to school on Monday?   _____ minutes

What are 3 possible reasons why Keith rides faster than Chris?

1. _____

2. _____

3. _____

Name _____

Strikes and Spares

Do you think that it is important to be a good bowler? _____

Why or why not? _____

_____

Bowling costs $3.65 a game. Shoes are $2.70 a pair. How much will it cost a family of 4 to bowl 3 games each?

$_____

If this ball and pin could talk, what would they say?

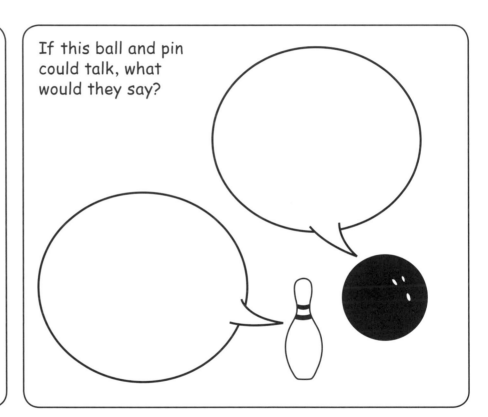

What are 4 things that you could use a bowling ball for besides bowling?

1. _____

2. _____

3. _____

4. _____

Critical and Creative Thinking Activities • EMC 3395 • © Evan-Moor Corp.

Strikes and Spares

Write a sentence about bowling. Use exactly 10 words.

_____

_____

Write a sentence using the words *ball*, *strike*, *pins*, and *spaghetti*.

_____

_____

Use the clues to find words that rhyme with either *BALL* or *PIN*.

holds the ceiling up   _____

holds your insides in   _____

season   _____

not short   _____

to turn around and around   _____

on a fish   _____

to use a phone   _____

on your face   _____

many stores together   _____

Shaun went bowling today. Use the clues to find out what his score was.

- Shaun's score was more than 100 but less than 135.

- The sum of the tens and the ones digits is 7.

- The score is <u>not</u> odd.

- The tens and the ones digits are consecutive.

Shaun's score: _____

Compose a short rhyming poem about bowling. Use the words *pin* and *win*.

_____

_____

Strikes and Spares

Can you get a strike? Use the numbers in the box to make an equation whose solution is the number on the pin. You may use **+**, **−**, **×**, and **÷**. Write the equation on the line and cross out the pin. You get one point for each pin you cross out. Be sure to record your score for each game.

1. $2 + 2 - 3 = 1$ _____
2. _____
3. _____
4. _____
5. _____
6. _____
7. _____
8. _____
9. _____
10. _____

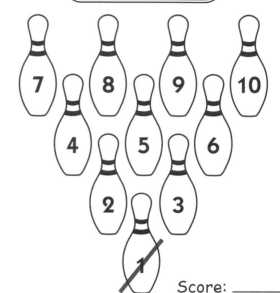

Score: _____

1. _____
2. _____
3. _____
4. _____
5. _____
6. _____
7. _____
8. _____
9. _____
10. _____

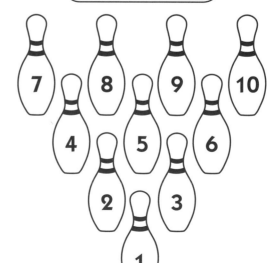

Score: _____

Name _____

Board Games

When you are learning a board game, do you like to read the directions or have someone explain the rules to you?

_____ Why? _____

_____

Think of 2 different board games. Write them on the lines. Then fill in the chart with 3 ways they are the same and 3 ways they are different.

Board games: _____ and _____

Same	Different

When you play a board game with 2 dice, you have a higher chance of rolling a 7 than any other number. Explain why you think this is true.

_____

_____

_____

What numbers do you have the lowest chance of rolling? _____ and _____

Why? _____

_____

Board Games

Use a different board game for each answer. Name a game that...

uses dice _____

has markers _____

uses money _____

requires math _____

involves strategy _____

has cards _____

requires a pencil _____

involves mostly luck _____

Who should put away the game?

☐ the loser

☐ the winner

☐ everyone who played

Why?

_____

_____

_____

_____

Do you think it is a good idea to let a little kid win a board game? _____

Why or why not? _____

_____

Read the clues and match each person with the game he or she likes the most.

• John's and Tim's favorite games use dice.

• The names of Sarah's and Marla's favorite games both have double letters in them.

• Sarah and Andrew are <u>not</u> good at spelling.

• John's game requires a pen or a pencil.

Monopoly: _____

Yahtzee: _____

Checkers: _____

Battleship: _____

Scrabble: _____

Name _____

Board Games

Write the names of the board games in the grid.

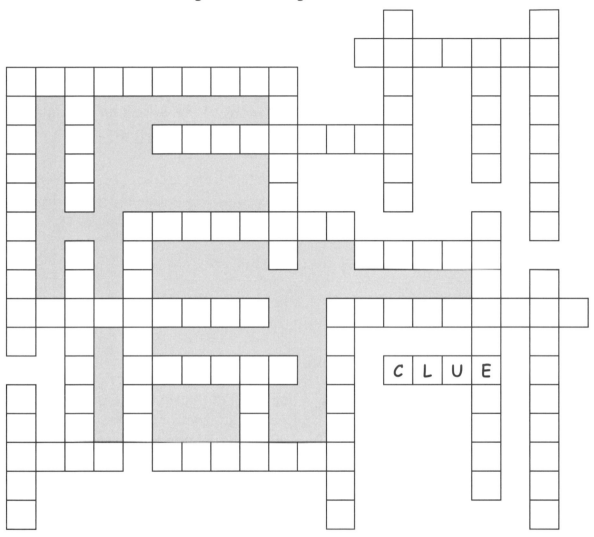

C L U E

4 Letters
~~CLUE~~
LIFE
RISK

5 Letters
BINGO
CHESS
JENGA
SORRY

6 Letters
BOGGLE

7 Letters
CRANIUM
OTHELLO
TROUBLE
YAHTZEE

8 Letters
CHECKERS
KERPLUNK
MONOPOLY
SCRABBLE
STRATEGO

9 Letters
CANDYLAND
MOUSETRAP
OPERATION
PARCHEESI

10 Letters
BATTLESHIP
PERFECTION
PICTIONARY

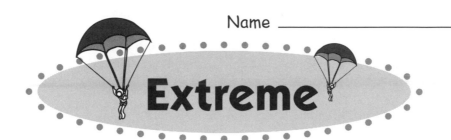

Extreme

Do you like extreme sports? Draw a ★ next to the sports that you have already tried. Write **D** next to the sports that you would **definitely** like to try. Write **M** next to the sports that you **might** want to try. Write **N** next to the sports that you would **not** want to try.

_____ snowboarding

_____ skateboarding

_____ in-line skating

_____ mountain biking

_____ rock climbing

_____ parasailing

_____ skydiving

_____ bungee jumping

_____ hang gliding

_____ surfing

_____ paintball

_____ stunt diving

_____ whitewater rafting

_____ windsurfing

_____ wakeboarding

Jen goes to the skate park every other day. Terry goes to the skate park every third day. Carlos goes to the skate park only on Mondays and Tuesdays. Today is Monday, June 3, and all 3 kids are at the skate park. On what date will they all be at the skate park again?

Day: _____

Date: _____

Eleven kids are at the skate park. Some of them have in-line skates (4 wheels per skate), some of them have skateboards (4 wheels), and some of them have bikes (2 wheels). There are 62 wheels altogether. How many kids are using each kind of equipment?

In-line skates: _____

Skateboards: _____

Bikes: _____

Name _____

Extreme

What is the main difference between a regular sport and an extreme sport?

_____

_____

Think of an extreme sport that you do <u>not</u> know much about. Write it on the line. Then write 3 questions you have about that sport.

Extreme sport: _____

1. _____

2. _____

3. _____

Extreme begins with *ex*. Use the clues to find other *ex* words.

where you leave	ex_____
a pro	ex_____
a spare	ex_____
to look around	ex_____
to get bigger	ex_____
to stretch the truth	ex_____

Josie loves to snowboard. She has decided to buy a season pass instead of purchasing daily lift tickets. Daily lift tickets cost $38. A season pass costs $475. If Josie goes snowboarding 16 times during the season, how much money will she save by purchasing a season pass instead of daily lift tickets?

$ _____

Complete the sentences.

_____ rock climbing _____.

_____ your mountain bike?

Snowboarding _____.

Extreme

Each of the kids listed below enjoys a different extreme sport. Each of them did his or her sport on a different day last week. Use the clues to find everyone's favorite sport and the day he or she did it. Make an **X** in a square when it <u>cannot</u> be an answer. Draw a circle when it is a correct answer. **Hint:** When you draw a circle in a square, you can make an **X** in all of the other squares in that row and column.

		Sports						Days					
		In-line skating	Snowboarding	Mountain biking	Surfing	Rock climbing	Skateboarding	Monday	Tuesday	Wednesday	Thursday	Friday	Saturday
Kids	Natalie												
	Brendan												
	Chandra												
	Jeremy												
	Anna												
	Donald												

1. Chandra and Jeremy do <u>not</u> need a board to do their sports. One of these two people was the first to do their sport this week and the other was the last.

2. None of the girls likes a sport that takes place in the water. None of the boys likes a sport that takes place in the snow.

3. Natalie did her sport the day before Chandra. Brendan did his sport the day after Jeremy.

4. Anna's sport takes twice as many wheels as Donald's sport. Jeremy's sport takes half as many wheels as Donald's sport.

5. The day after Anna did her sport, she went to watch Donald do his sport.

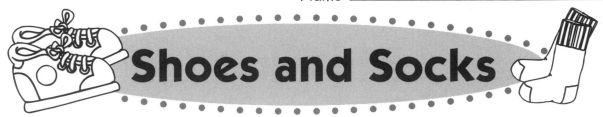

Shoes and Socks

Don't look! Answer the questions about your shoes without looking at them.

What size are your shoes? _____ Are they dirty? _____

What color are your shoes? _____

What are your shoes made out of? _____

What color are the bottoms of your shoes? _____

Now look at your shoes. Draw a ★ next to the answers you got right.

SIMILES

The shoes were as dirty as _____.

The dirty socks smelled like _____.

The shiny shoes looked like _____.

The socks were as white as _____.

Unscramble each kind of shoe. Then write who would wear it.

Scrambled Shoe	Unscrambled Shoe	Who Would Wear It
OKRW TOBOS		
LEBLAT PILPSRES		
LATSEC		
LADNSAS		
GHIH ELEHS		
UBRBRE BSOTO		

Shoes and Socks

Zack has 18 socks in his drawer. 6 of them are blue, 6 of them are red, and 6 of them are green. If Zack pulls socks out of his drawer without looking, how many socks will he have to pull out to make sure he gets a matched pair?

_____ socks

Today, Zack wants to wear blue socks. How many socks will he need to pull out to be sure that he gets a pair of blue socks?

_____ socks

There are 15 people in a room. 8 people are wearing socks, 6 people are wearing shoes, and 4 people are wearing both. How many people are barefoot?

_____ barefoot people

A man comes into the room and takes all the shoes and two pairs of socks. How many people are barefoot now?

_____ barefoot people

What does each expression mean?

"If I were in your shoes…" _____

_____

"The shoe's on the other foot now!" _____

_____

What do they say?

shoes **shoes**	**sock**	**MY**HOLE**SOCK**
_____	_____	_____

Shoes and Socks

Use the information in the box to answer the questions below.

soccer shoes
$26.30

cowboy boots
$38.90

high-tops
$27.90

snow boots
$28.20

slip-ons
$25.70

tap shoes
$23.80

running shoes
$34.50

pair of socks
$3.00

Darlene bought a pair of boots and a pair of shoes. She spent $54.50. What did she buy?

_____

_____

Annette bought 2 pairs of shoes and 2 pairs of socks. She spent $60.20. What shoes did she buy?

_____

_____

Tommy bought a pair of shoes and 3 pairs of socks. He spent $43.50. What shoes did he buy?

_____

Cubby bought a pair of boots and 2 pairs of shoes. He spent $92.50. What did he buy?

_____

_____

Bobby bought snow boots and slip-ons. How much did he spend? $_____

He paid with 3 twenty-dollar bills. How much change did he get back? $_____

You have $75.00. What will you buy? _____

How much change will you get back? _____

Name _____

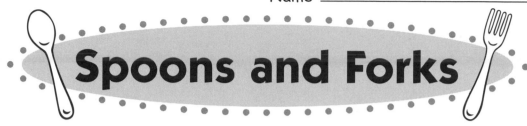

Spoons and Forks

If you could use <u>only</u> a spoon or a fork for the rest of your life, which would you choose?

_____ Why? _____

_____

What are 5 things that you could use a spoon or fork for besides eating?

Spoon	Fork
1. _____	1. _____
2. _____	2. _____
3. _____	3. _____
4. _____	4. _____
5. _____	5. _____

Use the clues to find words that rhyme with either *SPOON* or *FORK*.

in the night sky _____

ham or bacon _____

lunchtime _____

bottle stopper _____

in a little while _____

spun by a caterpillar _____

Myron is in charge of buying forks for the schoolwide spaghetti feed. He bought 8 cartons of plastic forks. Each carton contains 12 boxes. Each box contains 72 forks. How many plastic forks did Myron buy?

_____ plastic forks

Spoons and Forks

Write a sentence using the words *spoon*, *fork*, *eat*, and *mittens*.

_____

You want to eat soup, but you do not have a spoon, and you don't want to drink directly from the bowl (because that would be rude). What else could you use?

1. _____

2. _____

3. _____

Draw It:
There are 2 spoons and 1 fork.
The fork is between the spoons.
The tines of the fork are toward the top of the picture. The bowls of the spoons are toward the bottom.

Ms. Pettigrew collects fancy silver teaspoons. She obtains one new spoon on the first day of each month. She now has 446 spoons in her collection. How long has Ms. Pettigrew been collecting spoons?

_____ years and _____ months

Ms. Pettigrew displays her spoons in two kinds of glass cases. One kind holds 16 spoons, and the other kind holds 30 spoons. She has 20 cases altogether, and all the cases are full. How many of each kind of case does Ms. Pettigrew have?

Holds 30 spoons: _____

Holds 16 spoons: _____

Spoons and Forks

Help the ant get from one side of the table to the other. The ant must use the spoons and forks and must travel **spoon-fork-spoon-fork**. He must <u>not</u> travel over 2 spoons or 2 forks in a row.

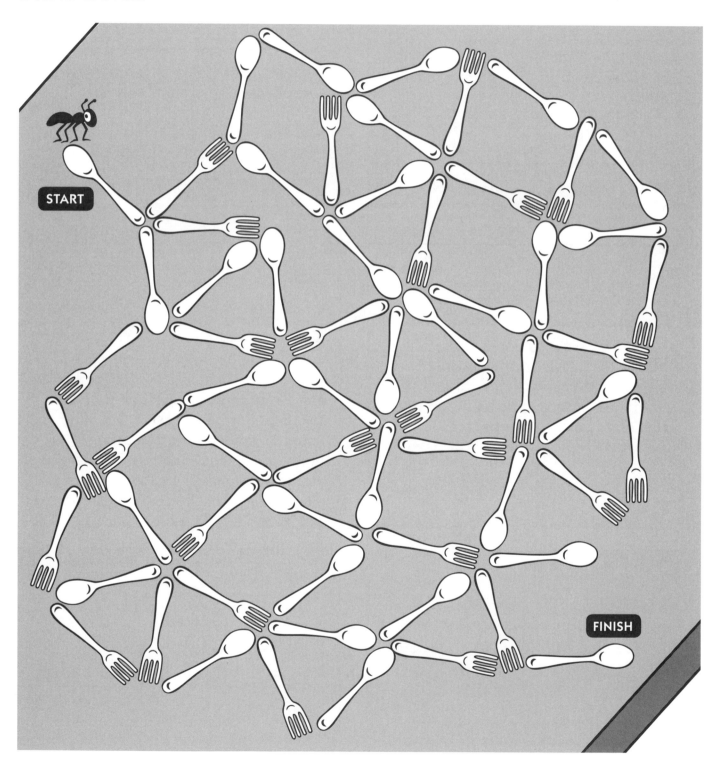

START

FINISH

Critical and Creative Thinking Activities • EMC 3395 • © Evan-Moor Corp.

Name _____

Wheels

The answer is **It had big wheels.** What is the question?

_____

Unscramble the things that have wheels, and then write the words in the grid.

ARC _____

TRAC _____

KRUCT _____

NARIT _____

GONAW _____

STESKA _____

CROTOES _____

LYCEBIC _____

RICCETLY_____

CRATTOR _____

TORKDABASE _____

CROEMCOTLY _____

HERLCAHEWI _____

Why do you think that most cars have 4 wheels instead of 3 or 5?

_____

_____

Wheels

What are 5 ways your life would be different if the wheel had never been invented?

1. _____

2. _____

3. _____

4. _____

5. _____

What does this phrase mean?

Do not reinvent the wheel.

_____

Find words around this wheel by following the rim and the spokes. You may <u>not</u> retrace your path, skip a letter, or use the same letter twice in one word. One is done for you.

1. lamb _____   10. _____

2. _____   11. _____

3. _____   12. _____

4. _____   13. _____

5. _____   14. _____

6. _____   15. _____

7. _____   16. _____

8. _____   17. _____

9. _____   18. _____

Name _____

Wheels

Each of the smaller wheels within the one big wheel below contains numbers that all have something in common. Write the commonality on the line in each wheel. In the overlapping section, write a number that can fit in both wheels. One is done for you.

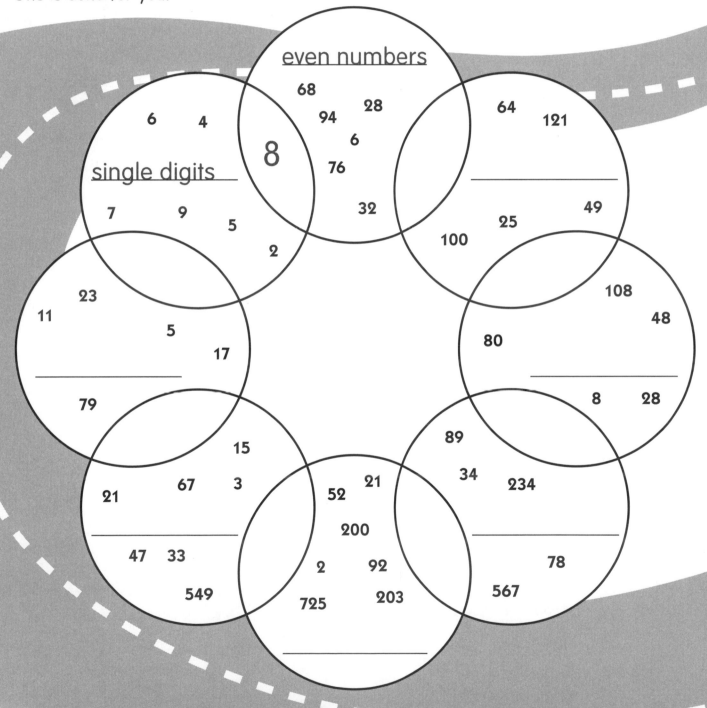

even numbers
68
94   28
6
76
32

single digits _____
6   4
7   9
5
2
8

64   121
_____
25   49
100

108
80   48
8   28

23
11
5
17
79

15
67   3
21
_____
47   33
549

89
34   234
_____
567   78

52   21
200
2   92
725   203
_____

Name _____

Remote Control

If you could have a special remote control that could control anything in the whole world, what would you want to be able to stop, rewind, fast-forward, and turn on and off?

_____ Why? _____

_____

Use the clues to find the words. The letters can all be found in *REMOTE CONTROL.*

on your foot _____

living or bed _____

for ice cream _____

engine _____

short letter _____

plant part _____

stolen money _____

ripped _____

hammer or wrench _____

Rodney owns Klicker Kingdom, a store that sells only remote controls. Last week, Rodney sold four and a half as many remote controls on Tuesday as he did on Wednesday. He sold 42 fewer remote controls on Thursday than he did on Tuesday. He sold 26 remote controls on Wednesday. How many did Rodney sell on Tuesday and Thursday?

Tuesday: _____

Thursday: _____

Most remote controls are black. Why do you think this is?

_____

_____

Name _____

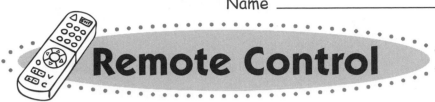

Remote Control

How do you think remote controls work?

_____

_____

The answer is **the remote control**. What are 3 questions?

1. _____

2. _____

3. _____

How many buttons are on Tony's new remote control? Read the clues to find out.

- The number of buttons is a prime number under 50.

- The sum of the digits is 10.

- The ones digit is 4 more than the tens digit.

There are _____ buttons.

List 4 things that can have remote controls besides TVs.

1. _____

2. _____

3. _____

4. _____

You have decided to play a joke on your family by hiding the TV remote.
Where would you hide it if you wanted them to...

find it quickly? _____

search for a while? _____

search all day? _____

Name _____

Remote Control

The word *remote* has an **r** and then a **t** in it. How many other words can you make that have both of those letters? The **r** <u>must</u> come before the **t**. Examples: *rate, bright*

r and t			

1. _____   8. _____   15. _____   22. _____

2. _____   9. _____   16. _____   23. _____

3. _____   10. _____   17. _____   24. _____

4. _____   11. _____   18. _____   25. _____

5. _____   12. _____   19. _____   26. _____

6. _____   13. _____   20. _____   27. _____

7. _____   14. _____   21. _____   28. _____

Now try **c** and **l**, like in the word *control*.

c and l			

1. _____   8. _____   15. _____   22. _____

2. _____   9. _____   16. _____   23. _____

3. _____   10. _____   17. _____   24. _____

4. _____   11. _____   18. _____   25. _____

5. _____   12. _____   19. _____   26. _____

6. _____   13. _____   20. _____   27. _____

7. _____   14. _____   21. _____   28. _____

   Critical and Creative Thinking Activities • EMC 3395 • © Evan-Moor Corp.

Name _____

How much money do you think a person has to have to be rich? _____

Underline one for each choice. Would you rather…

be smart **or** be rich?

have $500 right now **or** have $1,000 in a year?

get $100 every day for the rest of your life **or** get one million dollars right now?

be given $1,000 **or** have $10,000 given to the charity of your choice?

be poor and have a loving family **or** be rich and live alone?

It has been said that money can't buy happiness. What are 4 other things that money can't buy?

1. _____

2. _____

3. _____

4. _____

An American dollar bill is 6 inches long. A football field is 360 feet long. How many one-dollar bills would you have to line up end to end to reach from one end of a football field to the other?

_____ dollar bills

How much money would you have if they were twenty-dollar bills?

$_____

Minimum wage is the least amount of money that an adult can be paid per hour for doing a job. How much do you think minimum wage should be?

_____ Why? _____

_____

Name _____

Money

What does each expression about money mean?

"I feel like a million bucks." _____

_____

"Put your money where your mouth is." _____

_____

"Money doesn't grow on trees." _____

_____

What would happen if money really did grow on trees? _____

_____

Jolene has 3 times as many five-dollar bills as she does twenty-dollar bills. She has twice as many one-dollar bills as she does five-dollar bills. She has two fewer ten-dollar bills than five-dollar bills. She also has $3.57 in change. Jolene has two twenty-dollar bills. How much money does Jolene have altogether?

$_____

The U.S. Treasury is going to let you decide whose picture should appear on coins and bills. Write your choice for each one.

penny _____

nickel _____

dime _____

quarter _____

one-dollar bill _____

five-dollar bill _____

ten-dollar bill _____

twenty-dollar bill _____

Money

To solve each puzzle below, fill in the empty squares with letters for pennies (P), nickels (N), dimes (D), or quarters (Q). The total amount of money for each row and column must match the amounts given on the right side and bottom of the grid.

Q	N	P		D	.42
D		P	N	Q	.46
	D		D	P	.36
P	N	Q	N		.61
.41	.25	.37	.21	.61	

N		Q	N		.50
D		P		P	.27
	D	D		P	.47
Q	Q			N	.70
.65	.45	.41	.21	.22	

D				D	N	Q	Q	D	.88
N	N	P	D	Q	N		P		.67
Q		D	N		D	N	P	N	.96
	N	N	D	Q	N	N	D	N	.71
Q	N	D		N			P	D	.87
P	P		Q	D		P	Q	Q	.94
.67	.42	.28	.76	.85	.35	.47	.63	.60	

	D	P	Q		P	P	D		.84
D	P		N	N		D		D	.57
N		P	N	D	P		N	N	.67
		N	P	D	N	P	Q	Q	.83
N	N	P	Q	P		Q		Q	.97
D	N	Q			D	D	N		.80
.56	.41	.43	.66	.41	.27	.72	.51	.71	

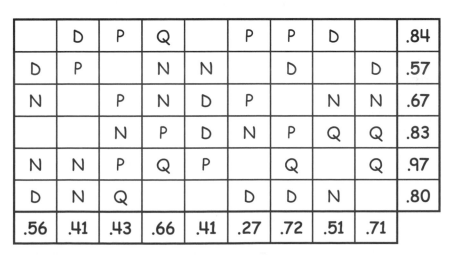

Name _____

Water

Where are 6 places you could find water in nature?

1. _____   3. _____   5. _____

2. _____   4. _____   6. _____

What are 6 things that you can put water in?

1. _____   3. _____   5. _____

2. _____   4. _____   6. _____

What are 6 things that you can use water for?

1. _____   3. _____   5. _____

2. _____   4. _____   6. _____

Your body is 70 percent water. A cup of water weighs about half a pound. About how many cups of water do you have in your body?

Your weight:

_____ pounds

Cups of water in your body:

_____

There are 3 identical pitchers in a row. The first one has twice as much water in it as the third one. The second one has one-third the amount of water as the first one. Draw the pitchers.

Water

It is always a good idea to conserve water. What are 3 things that you can do to use less water?

1. _____

2. _____

3. _____

About how much water do you think it would take to fill...

your shoe? _____

your desk? _____

the wastepaper bin? _____

your classroom? _____

You have 3 cups. Cup A is 1/4 full and can hold twice as much water as cup B. Cup B is full. Cup C is the same size as cup A and is empty. If the water from cups A and B was poured into cup C, how full would cup C be?

_____ full

You have 3 pitchers. Two will hold 5 cups of water each. One will hold 7 cups of water. You need exactly 4 cups of water. Describe how you can get exactly 4 cups. You may <u>not</u> fill a pitcher part way and just guess the amount.

_____

_____

_____

_____

_____

_____

Water

Read the directions below and cross off words and numbers to find 3 facts about the world's largest lake. Write the facts on the lines.

THE	EXIT	51	LARGEST	EAR	FATE	LAKE
EXACT	IN	DEER	4,687	THE	WORLD	RICE
IS	BAFFLE	LAKE	BAIKAL	STATE	CAKE	WHICH
LITTLE	IS	LETTUCE	LOCATED	TOAST	679	HAT
EXPERT	GREAT	IN	BACK	TAX	SIBERIA	BOX

_____

LAKE	ANGLE	BAIKAL	BAIT	IS	685	MANGO
FIX	5,370	CAN	FEET	CARROT	MIXER	DEEP
PRETZEL	WEIGHT	AND	SMALL	HOLDS	AID	20
PERCENT	MINI	DARE	OF	405	THE	DATE
EGGS	WORLD'S	EAGLES	SURFACE	TINY	FRESH	WATER

_____

THERE	ARE	APPLE	EXTRA	OVER	ALL	1,700
BEAR	827	DIFFERENT	EXCEL	BITSY	SPECIES	PIZZA
OF	ACE	EXTEND	PLANTS	CORN	FREIGHT	AND
SLATE	ANIMALS	PETITE	WAIT	IN	23	ABOUT
LAKE	PEAS	BAD	BAIKAL	85	SIX	PLATE

_____

- In each row, cross off the word that is closest to **A** in the alphabet.
- Cross off the words that have an **X** in them.
- Cross off the words that mean the opposite of *big*.
- Cross off the names of foods.
- Cross off the odd numbers.
- Cross off the words that rhyme with *late*.

Name _____

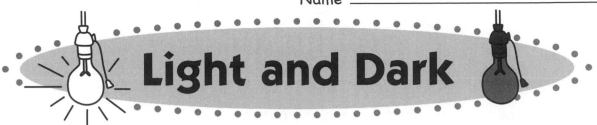

Light and Dark

How many different things can you think of that give off light?

1. _____ 4. _____ 7. _____

2. _____ 5. _____ 8. _____

3. _____ 6. _____ 9. _____

What are shadows? _____

_____

_____

Use the clues to find the words. The letters can all be found in *LIGHT* and *DARK*.

Scottish skirt _____

difficult _____

happy _____

ice from the sky _____

throw at a target _____

to speak _____

base of a sword _____

a bunny has a fluffy one _____

number 3 in line _____

Emilio has 27 light bulbs in his house. It costs him 4¢ in electricity for every hour that one bulb burns. If Emilio turns on every light in his house for 12 hours, how much will it cost him in electricity?

$ _____

Name _____

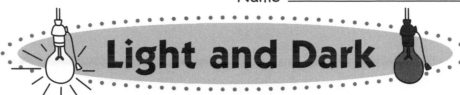

Light and Dark

What are 3 things that are hard to do in the dark?

1. _____

2. _____

3. _____

What are 3 things that are impossible to do in the dark?

1. _____

2. _____

3. _____

Big candles burn for 8 hours, and small candles burn for 3 hours. Joan burned one candle at a time for 49 hours. What is the lowest number of each size of candle that she could have?

_____ big candles

_____ small candles

It is December 21, the shortest day of the year. It got dark at 4:45 p.m. From now on, it will get dark 3 minutes later each day. On what date will it get dark at 6:00?

_____

Are you afraid of the dark? _____

Why or why not? _____

_____

_____

Name _____

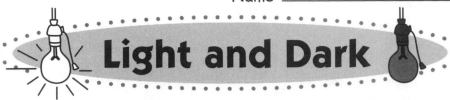

Light and Dark

Look at each grid with a shaded design. Then imagine how the design would look if the grid was turned 90 degrees to the right. Shade squares in the second grid to show how the design would look.

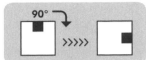

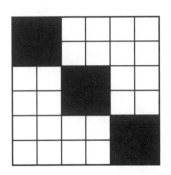 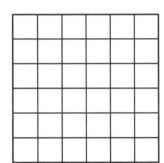 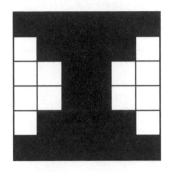 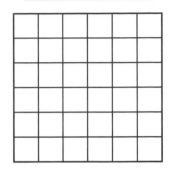

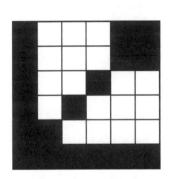 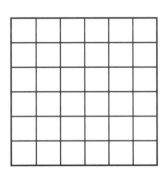  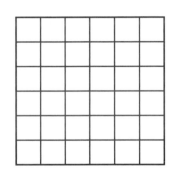

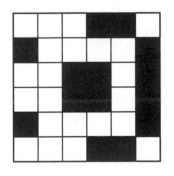 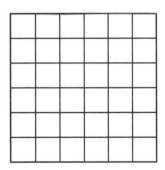 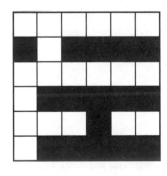 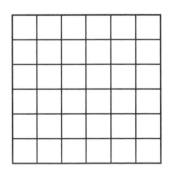

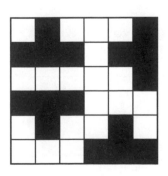 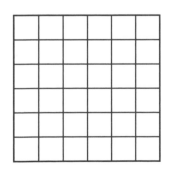 

Collections

Many people enjoy collecting things like shells or baseball cards. What are some other things that people collect?

1. _____   4. _____   7. _____

2. _____   5. _____   8. _____

3. _____   6. _____   9. _____

Why do you think people enjoy collecting things? _____

_____

Mark collects polished rocks. He has less than 35 of them. If he puts all of his rocks in two groups, there will be one left over. If he puts them in groups of three, there will be two left over. If he puts them in groups of four, there will be three left over. How many polished rocks are in Mark's collection?

_____ polished rocks

Sylvia collects marbles. The number of marbles she has is 3 digits. The digits are all consecutive, and if you add them, the sum will be 15. How many marbles does Sylvia have?

_____ marbles

A distant relative has left you his very valuable coin collection. What do you do with it?

_____

Why? _____

_____

Collections

Angela collects unicorn figurines. She keeps her favorite one on her nightstand. She put half of the remaining unicorns on her bookshelf. She keeps two-thirds of the rest on her desk. The remaining 6 unicorns are on her dresser. How many unicorns does Angela have?

_____ unicorns

Jordon collects baseball cards. He had 154 cards. Yesterday, he traded 16 of his less valuable cards for 3 special cards. Then he traded 7 more cards for 1 card. Then he bought a pack of 9 cards. How many baseball cards does Jordon have now?

_____ baseball cards

Jose used to collect sports pins, but then he stopped collecting and sold all of his pins. What are 3 possible reasons?

1. _____

2. _____

3. _____

Circle the letter of the statement that completes each syllogism.

All glass is breakable.

Most marbles are made from glass.

Therefore, _____.

A. all marbles are breakable

B. most marbles are breakable

C. some marbles are made from clay

All teddy bears are stuffed animals.

Some children collect teddy bears.

Therefore, _____.

A. some children collect stuffed animals

B. all children collect teddy bears

C. all stuffed animals are teddy bears

Collections

Many people collect state quarters. The quarters were issued in the order that each state was admitted to the Union. Color the states on the map below to show when each quarter was minted.

1999—Blue	2000—Yellow	2001—Light green	2002—Red	2003—Purple
Delaware	Massachusetts	New York	Tennessee	Illinois
Pennsylvania	Maryland	North Carolina	Ohio	Alabama
New Jersey	South Carolina	Rhode Island	Louisiana	Maine
Georgia	New Hampshire	Vermont	Indiana	Missouri
Connecticut	Virginia	Kentucky	Mississippi	Arkansas

2004—Brown	2005—Pink	2006—Light blue	2007—Green	2008—Orange
Michigan	California	Nevada	Montana	Oklahoma
Florida	Minnesota	Nebraska	Washington	New Mexico
Texas	Oregon	Colorado	Idaho	Arizona
Iowa	Kansas	North Dakota	Wyoming	Alaska
Wisconsin	West Virginia	South Dakota	Utah	Hawaii

If you had one quarter from each state, how much money would you have? $ _____

Name _____

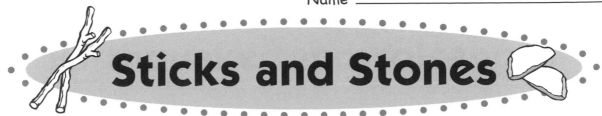

Sticks and Stones

You find a stick in the woods that is about 6 feet long. What are 6 different things that you could use it for?

1. _____   4. _____

2. _____   5. _____

3. _____   6. _____

Move just 3 sticks to make 3 identical squares. Cross off each stick you move and draw it in the new spot. **Hint:** It might help to use real toothpicks or matchsticks.

Change only the underlined letter in *STICK* or *STONE* to make a new word.

STICK _____

STICK _____

STONE _____

STONE _____

Now cross out just one letter in each word to make a new word.

STICK _____

STICK _____

STONE _____

Write a sentence using the words *sticks*, *stones*, *forest*, and *dishwasher*.

_____

_____

Name _____

Sticks and Stones

"Sticks and stones may break my bones, but words will never hurt me."

Do you think this is a true statement? _____

Why do you think so? _____

_____

_____

Use the clues to find other words that begin with *st*, like *sticks* and *stones*.

tale _____

to get ready for a test _____

smelly _____

church tower _____

to trip and fall _____

very hungry _____

pupil _____

artist's work space _____

horse's home _____

strong, hard metal _____

for trains or buses _____

make free of germs _____

There are 3 different sizes of stones. Fill in the number of medium-sized stones that belong on the bottom scale.

Critical and Creative Thinking Activities • EMC 3395 • © Evan-Moor Corp.

Sticks and Stones

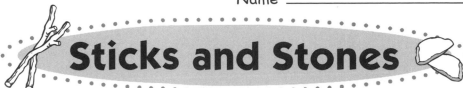

For each problem, read the clue, and then write how much the sticks and stones are worth. Make up your own for the last box.

Clue : Stones are worth twice as much as sticks.

🪨 + 🪵 = 96

Sticks = _____

Stones = _____

Clue : Sticks are worth twice as much as stones.

🪨 + 🪨 + 🪵 = 188

Sticks = _____

Stones = _____

Clue : Both are prime numbers. Sticks are greater.

🪨 × 🪵 + 🪨 = 84

Sticks = _____

Stones = _____

Clue : Stones are worth 3 more than sticks.

🪨 × 🪵 − 🪨 = 45

Sticks = _____

Stones = _____

Clue : Sticks are worth 3/4 of stones.

🪨 × 🪵 + 🪨 = 56

Sticks = _____

Stones = _____

Clue : _____

_____

Sticks = _____

Stones = _____

Name _____

Brothers and Sisters

Pretend that you are part of a large family with 6 brothers and 6 sisters. Fill in the chart with 3 advantages and 3 disadvantages of living in such a large family.

Advantages	Disadvantages

If it were up to you, would you be the oldest, the youngest, or an only child?

_____ Why? _____

_____

Make 4-letter words by using 2 letters from each of the words *BROTHER* and *SISTER*. Example: *toss*

B R O T H E R   S I S T E R

_____ _____   _____ _____

_____ _____   _____ _____

_____ _____   _____ _____

_____ _____   _____ _____

Write a sentence about brothers or sisters. Use exactly 8 words.

_____

Critical and Creative Thinking Activities • EMC 3395 • © Evan-Moor Corp.

Name _____

Brothers and Sisters

Complete each sentence.

My friend's little brother _____.

_____ your sister?

_____ two brothers _____.

Kyle is twice as old as his little brother and half as old as his big sister. Kyle's little brother is 12 years younger than his older sister. How old is Kyle?

_____ years old

In 3 years, Jennifer will be twice as old as her little sister. Jennifer's little sister is 3 years old now. How old is Jennifer now?

_____ years old

Brad has 4 brothers and sisters. Each one of his sibling's names contains 4 letters and begins with a letter in his name. Use the clues to find the names of Brad's siblings, and then write them in the chart.

B			
R			
A			
D			

- The first and the third names both contain double letters.

- The first and fourth are Brad's brothers while the second and third are his sisters.

- One of Brad's sisters is named after a flower, while the other sister's name is a palindrome (spelled the same forward and backward).

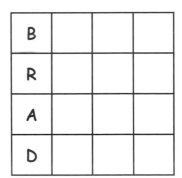

- The fourth name ends in the 7th letter of the alphabet. The second letter in the first name is an **I**.

Brothers and Sisters

There are 6 brothers and sisters in the Johnson family. Use the clues to find out how old each sibling is and in what month each one was born. Make an **X** in a square when it <u>cannot</u> be an answer. Draw a circle when it is a correct answer. **Hint:** When you draw a circle in a square, you can make an **X** in all of the other squares in that row and column.

		Ages					Months Born					
		5 years old	5 years old	8 years old	10 years old	11 years old	14 years old	January	April	April	June	October	November
Siblings	Paul												
	Carly												
	John												
	Tina												
	George												
	Janice												

1. John and Janice were both born in months that begin with the same letter as their names.

2. George's age is a double digit. It is also the same number as the month he was born in.

3. The twins are both girls.

4. The boy who is eight years old was born in November.

5. The oldest child is a boy. He was born in the sixth month of the year.

Windows and Doors

How many doors are in your house? _____

How many windows are in your house? _____

Most buildings are built with windows. Write 3 reasons for this.

1. _____

2. _____

3. _____

The Empire State Building in New York City has 6,500 windows! If it takes a window washer 7 minutes to wash each window, how many hours would it take to wash all of them? Round to the nearest hour.

_____ hours

Find the perimeter and the area of the entire window.

28

15

Perimeter: _____

Area: _____

Oh dear, you forgot to close the front door before you left your house today. What are 3 bad things that could happen?

1. _____

2. _____

3. _____

 Windows and Doors

Besides buildings, what are 5 other things that have doors?

1. _____

2. _____

3. _____

4. _____

5. _____

Windows are transparent. What are 5 other things that are transparent?

1. _____

2. _____

3. _____

4. _____

5. _____

What are 5 things you can see when you look out your bedroom window?

1. _____

2. _____

3. _____

4. _____

5. _____

When someone steps through the door to your house, what is the first thing you think he or she notices?

_____

_____

_____

Julia closed the window before she pulled the curtains. She let the cat out before she locked the door. She locked the door before she closed the window. In what order did Julia do those 4 things?

First: _____

Second: _____

Third: _____

Fourth: _____

Name _____

Windows and Doors

Complete each Word Window. Fill in the empty window pane with a letter that can be used with the other letters to make a word. Then write the word on the line. Use the letter in each box one time in your word.

R	
D	A

_____

	P
S	O

_____

	I
D	B

_____

E	
T	D

_____

	B
C	A

_____

H	N
	E

_____

V	E
T	

_____

A	
N	W

_____

E	☺	T
I	U	

_____

☺	V	E
	A	G

_____

W	R	E
	T	☺

_____

	N	I
E	D	R

_____

A	S	R
E	K	

_____

D	U	R
	O	A

_____

Read All About It!

What are 5 ways your life would be harder if you could not read?

1. _____

2. _____

3. _____

4. _____

5. _____

Number the things from 1 to 10 according to how much you would like to read them. The thing you would like to read the most should be number 1.

_____ newspaper

_____ scary story

_____ encyclopedia

_____ classic novel

_____ history book

_____ back of a cereal box

_____ magazine

_____ chapter book

_____ friend's web page

_____ biography

Ken has a goal to read one million words this year. If each page contains about 250 words, about how many pages will he need to read to attain his goal?

_____ pages

If the books Ken reads are about 200 pages long, how many books will he read?

_____ books

Name _____

Read All About It!

Sometimes books are made into movies (for example, *Charlotte's Web* or *Harry Potter*). Make a ✔ by the one you would rather do. Then write why on the lines.

☐ read the book first,   Why? _____
and then see the movie

_____

☐ see the movie first,
and then read the book   _____

☐ just read the book   _____

☐ just see the movie   _____

• • • • • • • • • • • • • • • • • • • •

What was the last book that you read? _____

Write 3 words to describe that book. _____, _____, _____

Summarize the book in one sentence. _____

_____

_____

How good was the book? Rate it by filling in 1 to 5 stars. ☆☆☆☆☆

What are the 5 best books you have ever read?

1. _____

2. _____

3. _____

4. _____

5. _____

Logan read 75 books last year.
40 percent of them were about
animals. How many animal books
did Logan read last year?

_____ animal books

Name _____

Each book in the stacks below was written by someone whose name has something to do with what he or she wrote about. Match the authors to the books by writing the correct number in the box next to each title.

1. Brock Lee

2. Dan Saul Knight

3. Dinah Sorus

4. Joe Kerr

5. Robin Banks

6. Ima Painter

7. Vic Tory

8. Mel Ting

9. Liza Wake

10. Ray King

11. Marcus Absent

12. Ira Fuse

13. Bill Ding

14. Nick L. Andime

15. Alec Tricity

16. Izzy Backyet

Great Artists ☐

Under Construction ☐

Prehistoric Giants ☐

Learn to Say "No" ☐

Learn to Tango ☐

Biography of a Comedian ☐

A Shocking Tale ☐

The Long Trip ☐

Crime Doesn't Pay ☐

The Long Hot Summer ☐

Be a Winner ☐

Cooking Vegetables ☐

Curing Insomnia ☐

Money Management ☐

Playing Hooky ☐

Yardwork For Dummies ☐

Name _____

Screen Time

Would you rather watch TV or use the computer? _____

Why?_____

_____

Number the kinds of TV shows from 1 to 8 according to how much you would want to watch them. The one you want to watch the most should be number 1.

_____ cooking show

_____ news

_____ game show

_____ sitcom

_____ cartoon

_____ nature program

_____ talk show

_____ reality show

During September, Katie used the computer for 45 minutes each day. During October, she used the computer for an hour each day. How many more hours did she use the computer in October than in September?

_____ hours

What is your favorite TV show?

_____

_____

About how much TV do you watch each week? _____

How much TV do you think a person your age should watch each week? _____

Why? _____

_____

_____

Screen Time

Why do you think the letters on a computer keyboard are not in alphabetical order?

_____

_____

Explain a television to someone who has never seen one.

_____

_____

_____

Jerome gets an hour of computer time each day. Make the circle into a pie chart to show how he uses his time. Be sure to label each section.

- Jerome spent 6 minutes watching a funny **video** about a cat and a toilet.

- He spent 10 minutes writing an **e-mail** to his grandma.

- He spent 15 minutes reading an **article** about tropical fish.

- He used 5 minutes to pick a new **screensaver**.

- He spent the rest of the time playing a **computer game**.

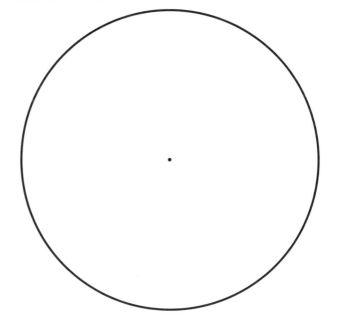

Write a sentence about watching TV. Use exactly 9 words.

_____

Screen Time

The left side of the chart below lists the top 20 TV shows for last week. In the center are some clues about where the shows ranked this week. Use the clues to list this week's top 20 TV shows on the right side of the chart.

Last Week		TOP 20 SHOWS	This Week	
Rank	Show	Clue	Rank	Show
1	American I-Sore	Down 2	1	
2	Name That Pickle	Down 8	2	
3	Gilligan's Toothpaste	Even number < 14	3	
4	Dancing with Dopey	Up 4	4	
5	The Last-Night Show	Up 1	5	
6	Dr. Empty	Odd number > 11	6	
7	560 Minutes	Up 5	7	
8	Bowling for Furniture	Prime number > 7	8	
9	The Obstructed View	Down 5	9	
10	Slugs in the City	Up 4	10	
11	Trading Faces	Tens + ones = 9	11	
12	What Not to Eat	Prime number < 6	12	
13	Extreme Homework	Down 7	13	
14	List Busters	Up 3	14	
15	Flint 48501	Symmetrical	15	
16	Project Runaway	Nearly last	16	
17	The Rachel L. Show	Up 10	17	
18	Desperate House Cats	Tens + ones = 8	18	
19	America's Funniest Hats	Even number	19	
20	Saturday Night Llamas	Odd number	20	

Pets

Oh dear, your new kitten is scratching the furniture! Write 3 ways to solve this problem. Draw a ★ by the one that you think would work best.

1. _____

2. _____

3. _____

Oh no! Your new puppy is making puddles everywhere! Write 3 ways to solve this problem. Draw a ★ by the one that you think would work best.

1. _____

2. _____

3. _____

In this word search, the names of 10 different kinds of pets are hidden two times each—once spelled forward and once backward. Use the chart to keep track of the pets you have found.

```
G O D F P A R R O T
G E R B I L N I G R
R E G I T S N A K E
S F Y B H M H N L T
T O R R A P U T M S
N C A W M X R S N M
A Z N V S U V H J A
C I A O T T P T H H
W Q C J E K A N S M
C A N A R Y O C I D
A K E L T R U T F O
T O R G L I B R E G
```

Kind of Pet Spelled Forward	Kind of Pet Spelled Backward

Pets

What are 3 reasons people have pets?

1. _____

2. _____

3. _____

Number the different pets from 1 to 12 according to how much you would like to have them. The one you would like the most should be number 1.	Number the pets from 1 to 12 again, this time according to how hard you think they would be to take care of. The hardest one should be number 1.
_____ hamster	_____ hamster
_____ parakeet	_____ parakeet
_____ lizard	_____ lizard
_____ dog	_____ dog
_____ snake	_____ snake
_____ guinea pig	_____ guinea pig
_____ horse	_____ horse
_____ fish	_____ fish
_____ turtle	_____ turtle
_____ cat	_____ cat
_____ parrot	_____ parrot
_____ ants	_____ ants

Pets

The 6 children listed below each have a different pet. Use the clues to find out which pet each child owns and what each pet's name is. Make an **X** in a square when it <u>cannot</u> be an answer. Draw a circle when it is a correct answer. **Hint:** When you draw a circle in a square, you can make an **X** in all of the other squares in that row and column.

		Pets						Pet Names					
		Dog	Cat	Hamster	Parakeet	Fish	Rabbit	Buddy	Happy	Sunshine	Doughnut	Flower	Cupcake
Children	Abby												
	Ben												
	Carrie												
	Daniel												
	Ella												
	Ford												

1. Ella's pet is bigger than Carrie's pet. Ella named her pet after her favorite food.

2. Abby's and Ben's pets are <u>not</u> mammals.

3. The cat, whose name is Flower, is <u>not</u> owned by a girl.

4. Sunshine and Happy do <u>not</u> have fur.

5. One child's name, type of pet, and pet's name all begin with the same letter.

6. The name of Abby's pet is <u>not</u> Happy, and her pet <u>cannot</u> swim.

Giggles

What are 3 things that make you laugh?

1. _____

2. _____

3. _____

What is something that often makes other people laugh but not you?

_____

Cole and Richard watched a funny movie. Cole laughed six times as many times as Richard did. The boys laughed 56 times altogether. How many times did each boy laugh?

Cole: _____

Richard: _____

A group of kids watched a cartoon. 36 of them thought it was very funny. Twice as many thought it was a little funny, and a fourth as many did not think it was funny at all. How many kids watched the cartoon?

_____ kids

You have a clown for a substitute teacher! What are 3 problems that you think he or she might have?

1. _____

2. _____

3. _____

Name _____

# Giggles

Fill in the blanks with words to make each sentence funny.

One day, a _____ frog jumped into a big _____.

My mother always says I should never _____ with my

_____.

The boys were late for _____ because they _____.

Use the clues to find things that can be funny. Cross out the letters you use on the right. Then unscramble the remaining letters to make a word that means the same thing as *giggle*.

big shoes, red nose	_____
animated TV show	_____
checked out at the library	_____
in the newspaper	_____
in a theater or on DVD	_____
tell one to a friend	_____

```
O  C  J  H  O  C  O  I  C  O
W  K  E  O  U  A  L  R  E  O
M  K  V  K  L  T  N  O  C  I
C  N  E  S  M  B  O  C
```

Letters left: __ __ __ __ __ __

Another word for *giggle* is:

_____

What do they have in common?

Lucy, Calvin, Garfield: _____

Banana peel, wet floor, soap: _____

Pilkey, Dahl, Seuss: _____

Write a funny sentence that has 6 words in it.

_____

Critical and Creative Thinking Activities • EMC 3395 • © Evan-Moor Corp.

Giggles

A spoonerism is a short phrase in which the initial sounds of the words have been switched, often with a humorous result. Find each spoonerism in the story and write the phrase correctly. The first one has been done for you.

One day, Timmy and his ~~sittle lister~~ **little sister** went to the playground. Timmy

climbed up a lig badder to go down the sleep stide. Then he and his sister

hug a dole in the sandbox. After that, Timmy climbed to the top of the

bonkey mars and slid down the pall tole. On the hay wome, Timmy and his sister

bopped sty the puck dond. They saw a dommy muck with her dellow yucklings.

● ● ● ● ● ● ● ● ● ● ● ● ● ● ● ● ●

Think of the spoonerism for each phrase. Then use it in a sentence.

water bottle _____

grilled cheese _____

math book _____

bubble gum _____

bake cookies _____

take a shower _____

Challenge: Write a sentence containing 2 spoonerisms that are not already on this page.

_____

_____

Emotions

What would make you feel...

happy? _____

frustrated? _____

nervous? _____

proud? _____

What are 6 ways you can make yourself feel better when you are feeling sad?

1. _____

2. _____

3. _____

4. _____

5. _____

6. _____

Claudia, Jamie, and Basil each made a list of things that make them happy. Jamie's list was 3 times as long as Basil's list. Claudia's list was half as long as Jamie's List. Together, Jamie's and Basil's lists were 120 things long. How long was each child's list?

Claudia: _____

Jamie: _____

Basil: _____

SIMILES

My mom was as angry as _____.

Our teacher was as surprised as _____.

The fear I felt was like _____.

The little boy was as sad as _____.

Name _____

Emotions

The answer is **excited!** What is the question?

_____

The answer is **homesick.** What is the question?

_____

When a person is very sad, he or she is depressed. What would a person be if he or she were very…

afraid _____

happy _____

angry _____

surprised _____

calm _____

brave _____

proud _____

nervous _____

annoyed _____

Nervous

This word looks nervous! Make the word *HAPPY* look happy and the word *ANGRY* look angry.

Draw a face in each circle to show the correct emotion.

 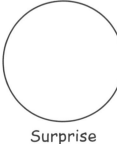 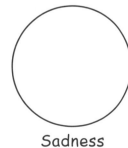 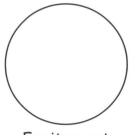 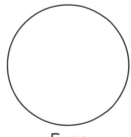

Anger   Surprise   Sadness   Excitement   Fear

Name _____

Emotions

Can you think of a way you could feel for each letter of the alphabet?
Try to write words for at least 20 of the letters.

A_____   N_____

B_____   O_____

C_____   P_____

D_____   Q_____

E_____   R_____

F_____   S_____

G_____   T_____

H_____   U_____

I_____   V_____

J_____   W_____

K_____   EX_____

L_____   Y_____

M_____   Z_____

Choose one of the emotions above and write it on the line.
Then use it to make as many smaller words as you can.   _____

1. _____   5. _____   9. _____

2. _____   6. _____   10. _____

3. _____   7. _____   11. _____

4. _____   8. _____   12. _____

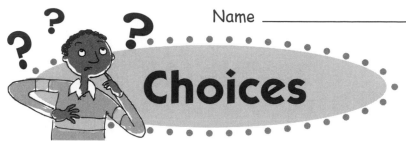

Choices

Every day, you make dozens of choices: what to wear, what to eat, where to sit. How many choices do you think you have made today? _____

What are 3 of those choices?

1. _____

2. _____

3. _____

Kristin has decided to paint every room in her house. She has chosen a different color of paint for each room. Read the clues and write the name of the color (**blue**, **green**, **yellow**, **purple**, or **orange**) she has picked for each room.

- The kitchen and the dining room are both primary colors.

- The bedroom is <u>not</u> orange.

- The colors of the dining room and the living room are both one-syllable words.

Kitchen: _____

Dining room: _____

Living room: _____

Bathroom: _____

Bedroom: _____

What is one of the most important choices you have ever made?

_____

What do you think will be 2 of the most important choices you'll make in the future?

1. _____

2. _____

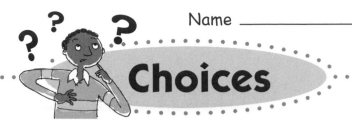

Name _____

Choices

Choose one word for each pair and circle it.

elephant **or** frog   table **or** chair   big **or** small   pen **or** crayon

Now write one sentence using all 4 of the words that you circled.

_____

_____

Try this fun math game!

Choose any number. _____

Add 3. _____

Multiply your result by 10. _____

Multiply your result
by your original number. _____

Subtract 10. _____

Divide by 10. _____

Add 1. _____

Divide by your original number. _____

Subtract 3 from the number. _____

Subtract your original number. _____

If you got 0, you did it right!

There are 4 different kinds of cookies in the big cookie jar. Each child chooses 3 different kinds of cookies. How many different combinations are possible?

_____ cookie combinations

What can you do if your friend makes an important choice that you do not agree with?

_____

_____

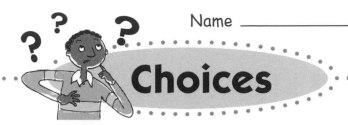

Name _____

Choices

Choose one, and then tell why you picked it.

Would you rather...

be a monkey **or** a hawk? _____

Why? _____

be a pencil **or** a stapler? _____

Why? _____

be an ice-cream bar **or** a carrot? _____

Why? _____

be able to turn invisible **or** to fly? _____

Why? _____

be super smart **or** super good-looking? _____

Why? _____

live for the rest of your life without TV **or** without junk food? ___

Why? _____

be good in school **or** good at sports? _____

Why? _____

Homework

Name _____

About how much homework do you do each day? _____

Do you think that amount is too much, too little, or about right? _____

Why do you think so? _____

_____

Charlotte can do 1 math problem in a minute and a half. There are 36 math problems on the homework page, but Charlotte has been assigned <u>only</u> the even-numbered ones. How long will it take her to complete her homework?

_____ minutes

Thomas started his homework at 7:43. At 8:18, he took an 8-minute break to have a snack. He finished his homework at 8:39. How long did Thomas spend doing homework?

_____ minutes

Krystal did her homework, but she did not turn it in. What are 3 possible reasons?

1. _____

2. _____

3. _____

Write a sentence using the words *homework*, *pencil*, *easy*, and *goat*.

_____

_____

Critical and Creative Thinking Activities • EMC 3395 • © Evan-Moor Corp.

Homework

You get to assign your class homework today, but you <u>must</u> follow these rules:

- The assignment you give should take about as long as your usual homework does.

- It must involve paper and a pen or pencil.

- It must be challenging.

Subject: _____   Homework assignment: _____

_____

What would your classmates learn from doing this assignment? _____

_____

• • • • • • • • • • • • • •

What kind of homework does Benjamin have tonight? Follow the directions and rewrite the word on each new line until you find out.

	B	E	N	J	A	M	I	N
Make the third letter the same as the second letter.								
Change the sixth letter to the vowel that is in both *STRAIGHT* and *STRIKE*.								
Change the first letter to the letter that comes before **T** in the alphabet.								
Change the last letter to the seventh letter in the alphabet.								
Change the fourth and fifth letters to **L**.								
Change the seventh letter to the letter that is in both *PENCIL* and *GROWN*.								
Change the second letter to the letter that comes before **Q** in the alphabet.								

Homework

Name _____

Homework is a compound word. Find your way through the puzzle below by forming compound words from one box to the next. You may move up, down, or across, but <u>not</u> diagonally. Start with *HOME* in the upper-left corner and end with *LAND* in the lower-right corner.

HOME	RUN	WAY	WRONG	BLUE	GREEN	APPLE	BEST
WORK	OUT	SIDE	HAPPY	FACE	OFF	PIE	FRIEND
HARD	KEY	LINE	DOWN	TOWN	HALL	HOME	SHIP
UP	HOLE	UP	STAIRS	LIGHT	SWITCH	PLATE	COUNT
TOP	HAT	HOLD	OVER	NIGHT	MARE	COLT	HOOF
TEA	SPOON	MIX	GOAT	STAND	UP	CHUCK	IN
CUP	SEE	MATCH	COOLER	OFF	THERE	PAPER	ROCK
RED	FREE	FALL	WATER	SPRING	TIME	SHARE	OUT
CLOUD	BURST	BACK	FRONT	SUN	BEAM	WARE	SHIRT
BIRD	BLACK	PACK	RAT	BOOK	CASE	PHONE	HOME
WING	SHOE	HORSE	POWER	HOUSE	BREAK	DOWN	FRONT
TALL	SHINE	ON	LIGHT	BOAT	OUT	TURN	ABOUT
TREE	HILL	TOP	OUT	HAND	OFF	OVER	COMIC
HOUSE	DOOR	KNOB	SIDE	WAYS	SHIRT	STOCK	BOOK
GRASS	MAT	RUG	BOX	CAR	OPEN	YARD	SALE
CART	WHEEL	TUG	BOY	POOL	HOUSE	STICK	BALL
ANT	MINT	BOAT	BUBBLE	GUM	FILE	WAY	PARK
HILL	BAR	MAN	KIND	MEAL	WORK	SNACK	LAND

Answer Key

Many of the questions in this book are open-ended, and students' answers will vary. Sample responses are provided for most of these activities. Accept any reasonable responses.

Page 5

Page 6

Page 7

Page 8

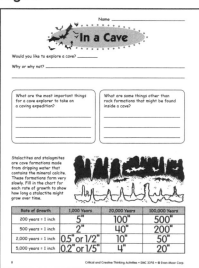

Page 9

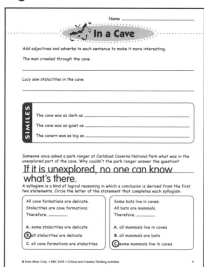

Page 10

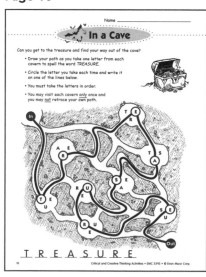

Page 11 — In the Desert

You are going for a hike in the desert. You can take only 3 of the things listed below. Circle them.

water · snack · sand toys · sunblock · hot · sunglasses · snakebite kit · compass

Joe's jeep can hold 25 gallons of gas in its tank, plus Joe has an extra tank that will hold another 25 gallons. His jeep can go 23 miles on 1 gallon of gas. He wants to cross a desert that is 1,200 miles long. Will Joe make it?

No, he will use just over 52 gallons and he has only 50.

A man is lost in the desert. He is out of water. He finds a water hole, but he does not drink from it. List 3 possible reasons.

1. _____
2. _____
3. _____

Circle the letter of the statement that completes each syllogism.

Some lizards live in the desert. All lizards are reptiles. Therefore, _____
A. all reptiles live in the desert
B. some lizards are reptiles
C. some reptiles live in the desert

All deserts have little water. The Sahara is a desert. Therefore, _____
A. the Sahara has little water
B. the Sahara is the desert
C. all deserts have sand

Page 12 — In the Desert

Use the clues to find things that are in a desert.

prickly plant — **cactus**
not really there — **mirage**
reptile — **snake**
on the ground — **sand**
stinging, spiderlike — **scorpion**
reptile — **lizard**

What are 6 words that describe the desert?
1. _____
2. _____
3. _____
4. _____
5. _____
6. _____

Write a sentence that is always true about deserts.
_____

Write a sentence that is sometimes true about deserts.
_____

Write a sentence that is never true about deserts.
_____

DRAW IT:
• There are 3 cactus plants.
• The cactus in the middle is the tallest. The one on the left is smaller than the one on the right, which has 2 red flowers.
• There is a bird on the smallest cactus.

Page 13 — In the Desert

To get through the desert, you must follow the cactus trail. Draw a path that spells the word CACTUS again and again. You may go up, down, or to either side, but not diagonally. The trail starts with the C in the upper-left corner and ends with the S in the lower-right corner.

Cactus Trail Challenge: Find the names of 3 animals that live in the desert.
1. **snake** 2. **scorpion** 3. **lizard**

Page 14 — In the Water

Which do you like better, swimming in a pool or swimming in a lake? _____
Why? _____

Number the water activities from 1 to 9 to show how much you would like to do them. The one you want to do the most should be number 1.
_____ diving off the high dive
_____ jumping off the high dive
_____ going down a waterslide
_____ diving for things underwater
_____ swimming laps
_____ jumping off the low dive
_____ diving off the low dive
_____ racing a friend across the pool
_____ doing somersaults and headstands

Emma swims faster than Maria. Maria swims slower than Amy. Drew swims slower than Emma.

Write T if the statement is true, F if it is false, and C if you cannot tell.
C Maria is the slowest.
C Amy swims faster than Drew.
F Drew is the fastest.
C Emma swims faster than Drew and Amy.
C Emma and Amy swim at the same speed.

SIMILES
The water was as cold as _____
The children splashed like _____
The pool was as crowded as _____

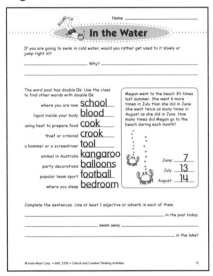

Page 15 — In the Water

If you are going to swim in cold water, would you rather get used to it slowly or jump right in?
_____ Why? _____

The word *pool* has double Os. Use the clues to find other words with double Os.
where you are now — **school**
liquid inside your body — **blood**
using heat to prepare food — **cook**
thief or criminal — **crook**
a hammer or a screwdriver — **tool**
animal in Australia — **kangaroo**
party decorations — **balloons**
popular team sport — **football**
where you sleep — **bedroom**

Megan went to the beach 34 times last summer. She went 6 more times in July than she did in June. She went twice as many times in August as she did in June. How many times did Megan go to the beach during each month?
June: **7**
July: **13**
August: **14**

Complete the sentences. Use at least 1 adjective or adverb in each of them.
_____ in the pool today.
_____ swam away _____ in the lake?

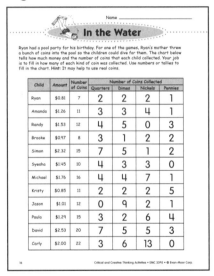

Page 16 — In the Water

Ryan had a pool party for his birthday. For one of the games, Ryan's mother threw a bunch of coins into the pool so the children could dive for them. The chart below tells how much money and the number of coins that each child collected. Your job is to fill in how many of each kind of coin was collected. Use numbers or tallies to fill in the chart. Hint: It may help to use real coins.

Child	Amount	Number of Coins	Quarters	Dimes	Nickels	Pennies
Ryan	$0.81	7	2	2	2	1
Amanda	$1.26	11	3	3	4	1
Randy	$1.53	12	4	5	0	3
Brooke	$0.97	8	3	1	2	2
Simon	$2.32	15	7	5	1	2
Syesha	$1.45	10	4	3	3	0
Michael	$1.76	16	4	4	7	1
Kristy	$0.85	11	2	2	2	5
Jason	$1.01	12	0	9	2	1
Paula	$1.29	15	3	2	6	4
David	$2.53	20	7	5	5	3
Carly	$2.00	22	3	6	13	0

Number of Coins Collected spans the Quarters, Dimes, Nickels, and Pennies columns.

Page 17 — At the Ice-Cream Store

What is the yummiest flavor of ice cream that you can think of? _____
What is the yuckiest flavor of ice cream that you can think of? _____

Karly is making a banana split. Number the steps from 1 to 10. The first step should be number 1.
6 Scoop the ice cream.
8 Add whipped cream.
3 Cut the banana.
9 Add sprinkles.
1 Get a bowl.
10 Eat it up!
4 Put the banana in the bowl.
7 Add chocolate sauce.
5 Get a spoon.
2 Peel the banana.

There are 2 kinds of cones: sugar and waffle. There are 3 flavors of ice cream: chocolate, vanilla, and strawberry. There are 3 toppings: sprinkles, nuts, and mini M&M's. How many different combinations of 1 cone, 1 scoop of ice cream, and 1 topping can you make?
18 combinations

How many combinations would there be if there were 4 flavors of ice cream?
24 combinations

The answer is chocolate ice cream. Write 3 different questions.
1. _____
2. _____
3. _____

Page 18 — At the Ice-Cream Store

Write a sentence using the words ice cream, paid, hot fudge, and baseball.
_____

Use the phone keypad to decode the ice-cream flavors. Remember, numbers 2 through 9 can represent one of 3 or 4 different letters. Example: 243779 = CHERRY
8264552 — **vanilla**
282253 486 — **bubble gum**
76259 7623 — **rocky road**
7872923779 — **strawberry**
246265283 2447 — **chocolate chip**

Jim owns an ice-cream store. Use the clues to find out how many ice-cream cones he sold last week.
• He sold more than 300 but fewer than 350.
• The last digit is odd.
• The second digit is 3 less than the last digit.
• The sum of the first 2 digits equals the last digit.
• The sum of all the digits is 14.
Jim sold **347** ice-cream cones.

Everybody is talking about Jim's new ice-cream flavor, Triple Chocolate Dream. Each day, his sales for this flavor have tripled! How many scoops did Jim sell on each day?
Monday: 1 scoop
Tuesday: **3** scoops
Wednesday: **9** scoops
Thursday: **27** scoops
Friday: **81** scoops
Saturday: **243** scoops!

Page 19 — At the Ice-Cream Store

Coach Clark took his team out for ice cream. Each player got a double-scoop cone and ordered a different combination of flavors than his teammates. There were 6 flavors of ice cream to choose from and 15 players on the team. Use the key to color the cones to show the 15 different combinations.

Chocolate ...... Brown
Strawberry ... Pink
Blueberry ...... Blue
Lemon .... Yellow
Pistachio .... Light Green
Sherbet .... Orange

Critical and Creative Thinking Activities • EMC 3395 • © Evan-Moor Corp.

Page 20

Name _____

In the Kitchen

What are 5 things that you know how to make in the kitchen?

1. _____
2. _____
3. _____
4. _____
5. _____

8 ounces = 1 cup
16 tablespoons = 1 cup

How many ounces in ¼ cup? **2**

How many tablespoons in ¼ cup? **4**

How many ounces in 4¼ cups? **34**

How many tablespoons in 6½ cups? **104**

This little story is full of homophones. Whenever you ~~see~~ one ~~sea won~~, cross it off and ~~write~~ the correct word above it.

The ~~Knight~~ Night Dad ~~Maid~~ Made Dinner
It was ~~thyme~~ time for ~~two~~ to make dinner. First, he put the ~~meatloaf~~ meatloaf in the oven. Then he peeled the potatoes and sliced the ~~beets~~ beets. The ~~beets~~ beets ~~made~~ his cutting ~~board~~ board red. He put ~~carrots~~ carrots, celery, and tomatoes ~~in~~ the salad. ~~There~~ was ~~a four dessert~~. Dinner was ~~great~~ great! After dinner, the ~~hole~~ whole family helped ~~two~~ to clean up the kitchen. Dad said that he ~~would~~ cook again next ~~week~~.

SIMILES

The fridge was as full as _____

The pans clattered like _____

The kitchen was as messy as _____

20 · Critical and Creative Thinking Activities · EMC 3395 · © Evan-Moor Corp.

Page 21

Name _____

In the Kitchen

Write 2 things in your kitchen for each letter.

S _____ and S _____
P _____ and P _____
M _____ and M _____
R _____ and R _____
G _____ and G _____
T _____ and T _____

Circle the one in each pair that would be hardest to live without.

stove or refrigerator
forks or spoons
plates or bowls
dishwasher or microwave
chairs or tables

Complete the sentences.

_____ in the kitchen?

The refrigerator _____

_____ the stove

Add one more to each list.

mixing bowl, measuring cup, flour sifter, _____
spoon, fork, plate, _____
spatula, rubber scraper, wire whisk, _____
blender, crockpot, coffee maker, _____
sage, basil, cinnamon, _____
steamer, soup pot, teakettle, _____

Aubrey made 3 dozen cookies. Half have raisins. 30 have nuts. If no cookies are plain, how many have both raisins and nuts?

12

© Evan-Moor Corp. · EMC 3395 · Critical and Creative Thinking Activities · 21

Page 22

Name _____

In the Kitchen

Use the clues to solve the crossword puzzle. The answers are things you would find in a kitchen.

Across: SINK, POT, MEASURINGCUP, LADLE, BOWL, PITCHER, SALT, SPOON, REFRIGERATOR, TOASTER
Down: SPATULA, KNIFE, OVEN, BLENDER, MILK, STOVE

ACROSS
1. Get water here
3. Make soup in this
5. Use to get just the right amount of milk
7. For serving punch or soup
9. Eat cereal in this
12. Fill with juice
13. In a shaker
14. Eat soup with this
16. Where the milk is
17. For browning bread

DOWN
1. For flipping pancakes
2. Be careful! Don't cut yourself.
4. Bake cookies in this
6. Use to take the outside off
8. Smoothie, please
9. Ding! Food's ready!
10. Make an omelet in this
11. The burners are hot!
15. Eating utensil with points

22 · Critical and Creative Thinking Activities · EMC 3395 · © Evan-Moor Corp.

Page 23

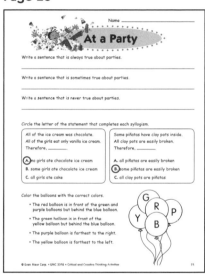

Name _____

At a Party

Write a sentence that is always true about parties.

_____

Write a sentence that is sometimes true about parties.

_____

Write a sentence that is never true about parties.

_____

Circle the letter of the statement that completes each syllogism.

All of the ice cream was chocolate.
All of the girls eat only vanilla ice cream.
Therefore,
(A) no girls ate chocolate ice cream
B. some girls ate chocolate ice cream
C. all girls ate cake

Some piñatas have clay pots inside.
All clay pots are easily broken.
Therefore,
A. all piñatas are easily broken
(B) some piñatas are easily broken
C. all clay pots are piñatas

Color the balloons with the correct colors.

- The red balloon is in front of the green and purple balloons but behind the blue balloon.
- The green balloon is in front of the yellow balloon but behind the blue balloon.
- The purple balloon is farthest to the right.
- The yellow balloon is farthest to the left.

(G R P / Y B)

© Evan-Moor Corp. · EMC 3395 · Critical and Creative Thinking Activities · 23

Page 24

Name _____

At a Party

Add adjectives and adverbs to make the sentences more interesting.

The girl ate cake at the party.

The piñata broke, and the children scrambled to get the candy.

Use the clues to find things that might be at a party.

Pop! B **alloon**
blow them out C **andles**
musical chairs G **ame**
full of candy P **iñata**
don't let it melt I **ce cream**
open them P **resents**
for dancing M **usic**
on your head H **at**

How many people came to the block party? Use the clues to find out.

- There were more than 50 people but fewer than 60.
- There were an odd number of kids and an odd number of adults.
- The tens digit is a higher number than the ones digit.
- The sum of the digits is 9.

54 people

Explain a birthday party to someone who has never heard of one.

_____

24 · Critical and Creative Thinking Activities · EMC 3395 · © Evan-Moor Corp.

Page 25

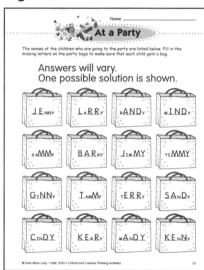

Name _____

At a Party

The names of the children who are going to the party are listed below. Fill in the missing letters on the party bags to make sure that each child gets a bag.

Answers will vary.
One possible solution is shown.

JE**NNY** L**A**RR**Y** **R**AND**Y** **M**IND**Y**
S**A**MM**Y** BARR**Y** J**I**MMY **TI**MMY
G**I**NN**Y** **TA**MM**Y** **T**ERR**Y** SAND**Y**
C**I**ND**Y** KERR**Y** **M**AND**Y** KENN**Y**

© Evan-Moor Corp. · EMC 3395 · Critical and Creative Thinking Activities · 25

Page 26

Name _____

At a Carnival

Would you rather ride the Ferris wheel or the roller coaster?

Why? _____

Elly and Sharon bought tickets for the Ferris wheel, but they did not go on the ride. Give 3 possible reasons.

1. _____
2. _____
3. _____

Rides cost 2, 3, or 4 tickets. Rob had 25 tickets. He went on 9 rides and had one ticket left over. How many of each kind of ride did Rob go on?

2-ticket rides: **5**
3-ticket rides: **2**
4-ticket rides: **2**

Circle 3 words that best describe your favorite kind of carnival ride.

slow   scary   spinning
dark   jerky   exciting
fast   high   unpredictable
loud   gentle   upside-down

Write an interrogatory sentence about the carnival.

_____

Write an exclamatory sentence about the carnival.

_____

Write a sentence about the carnival that contains quotation marks.

_____

26 · Critical and Creative Thinking Activities · EMC 3395 · © Evan-Moor Corp.

Page 27

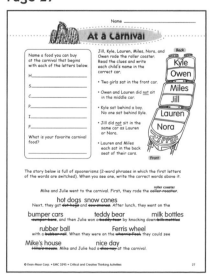

Name _____

At a Carnival

Name a food you can buy at the carnival that begins with each of the letters below.

H _____
S _____
C _____
P _____
I _____
F _____

What is your favorite carnival food?

Jill, Kyle, Lauren, Miles, Nora, and Owen rode the roller coaster. Read the clues and write each child's name in the correct car.

Back
Kyle
Owen
Miles
Jill
Lauren
Nora
Front

- Two girls sat in the front car.
- Owen and Lauren did not sit in the middle car.
- Kyle sat behind a boy. No one sat behind Kyle.
- Jill did not sit in the same car as Lauren or Nora.
- Lauren and Miles each sat in the back seat of their cars.

The story below is full of spoonerisms (2-word phrases in which the first letters of the words are switched). When you see one, write the correct words above it.

Mike and Julie went to the carnival. First, they rode the ~~coller roaster~~ roller coaster. Next, they got ~~sot hogs~~ hot dogs and ~~cow snones~~ snow cones. After lunch, they went on the ~~cumper bars~~ bumper cars, and then Julie won a ~~beddy tear~~ teddy bear by knocking down ~~bilk mottles~~ milk bottles with a ~~bubber rall~~ rubber ball. When they were on the ~~wherris feel~~ Ferris wheel, they could see ~~Mike's house~~ Mike's house. Mike and Julie had a ~~dice nay~~ nice day at the carnival.

© Evan-Moor Corp. · EMC 3395 · Critical and Creative Thinking Activities · 27

Page 28

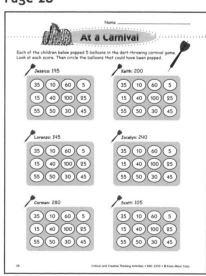

Name _____

At a Carnival

Each of the children below popped 5 balloons in the dart-throwing carnival game. Look at each score. Then circle the balloons that could have been popped.

Jessica: 195

35 10 60 5
15 40 100 25
55 50 30 45

Keith: 200

35 10 60 5
15 40 100 25
55 50 30 45

Lorenzo: 145

35 10 60 5
15 40 100 25
55 50 30 45

Jocalyn: 240

35 10 60 5
15 40 100 25
55 50 30 45

Carmen: 280

35 10 60 5
15 40 100 25
55 50 30 45

Scott: 105

35 10 60 5
15 40 100 25
55 50 30 45

28 · Critical and Creative Thinking Activities · EMC 3395 · © Evan-Moor Corp.

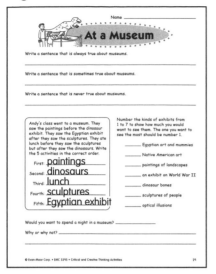

Page 30

Page 31

Page 32

Page 33

Page 34

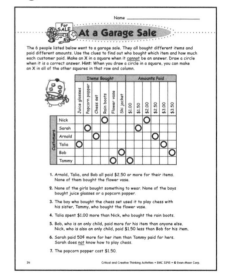

Page 35

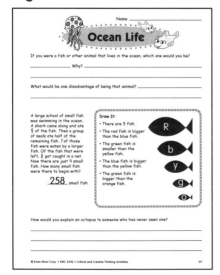

Page 36

Page 37

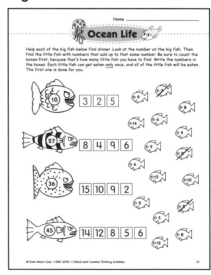

Critical and Creative Thinking Activities • EMC 3395 • © Evan-Moor Corp.

Page 38

Rain, Rain

What does it mean when someone says it is "raining cats and dogs"? _____

What are some other things it could be raining?	Draw one of the things it could be raining.
____ and ____	
____ and ____	
____ and ____	
____ and ____	
____ and ____	

Use the clues to find the words. Each word rhymes with *RAIN*.

cars on a track	**train**
spot on clothing	**stain**
in the bathtub	**drain**
country in Europe	**Spain**
connected rings	**chain**
in your head	**brain**
undecorated	**plain**

It is raining and you do not want to get your hair wet. You don't have an umbrella, a hat, or a hood. What are 6 other things you could use?

1. ____
2. ____
3. ____
4. ____
5. ____
6. ____

Page 39

Rain, Rain

Complete each sentence.

The rain _____!

_____ your umbrella _____

_____ rain boots?

Number the kinds of rain from 1 to 4. The lightest should be number 1 and the heaviest should be number 4.

3 shower
1 mist
4 downpour
2 drizzle

It rained more on Friday than it did on Sunday.
It rained less on Saturday than it did on Sunday.
It rained more on Monday than it did on Sunday.
Write T if the statement is true, F if it is false, and C if you cannot tell.

T More rain fell on Monday than on Saturday.
C More rain fell on Friday than on Monday.
C The least amount of rain fell on Saturday.
C It rained the same amount on Friday and Monday.

Circle the letter of the statement that completes each syllogism.

Red is a bright color. Some umbrellas are red. Therefore,	All plants need rain. Some plants are trees. Therefore,
A. all umbrellas are a bright color	Ⓐ all trees need rain
Ⓑ some umbrellas are a bright color	B. some trees need rain
C. all umbrellas are red	C. all plants are trees

Page 40

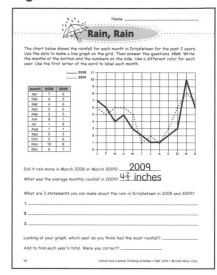

Rain, Rain

The chart below shows the rainfall for each month in Drizzletown for the past 2 years. Use the data to make a line graph on the grid. Then answer the questions. **Hint:** Write the months at the bottom and the numbers on the side. Use a different color for each year. Use the first letter of the word to label each month.

Month	2008	2009
Jan	7	6
Feb	6	5
Mar	4	6
Apr	5	6
May	3	5
Jun	2	1
Jul	2	1
Aug	1	1
Sep	2	3
Oct	3	6
Nov	10	8
Dec	6	7

Did it rain more in March 2008 or March 2009? **2009**

What was the average monthly rainfall in 2009? **4 2/4 inches**

What are 3 statements you can make about the rain in Drizzletown in 2008 and 2009?

1. ____
2. ____

Looking at your graph, which year do you think had the most rainfall? ____

Add to find each year's total. Were you correct? ____

Page 41

Sunshine

Without the sun, there could be no life on Earth. What are 5 different ways that people benefit from the sun?

1. ____
2. ____
3. ____
4. ____
5. ____

The sun is about 93 million miles from the Earth. If you went to the sun in a heatproof rocket that traveled at a rate of 5,000 miles per hour, how long would it take you to get there?	It was 6 degrees hotter on Friday than it was on Saturday. On Sunday, it was 11 degrees cooler than it was on Friday. On Saturday, it was 79 degrees. How hot was it on Friday and Sunday?
In hours: **18,600**	
In days: **775**	
About how many years is that?	Friday: **85°**
2	Sunday: **74°**

SIMILES

The hot sand was like ____
The sun was as bright as ____
The girl's sunburn was as red as ____

Page 42

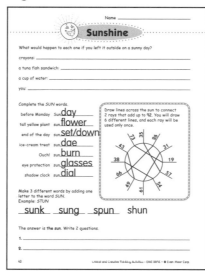

Sunshine

What would happen to each one if you left it outside on a sunny day?

crayons: ____

a tuna fish sandwich: ____

a cup of water: ____

you: ____

Complete the *SUN* words.

before Monday	sun**day**
tall yellow plant	sun**flower**
end of the day	sun**set/down**
ice-cream treat	sun**dae**
Ouch!	sun**burn**
eye protection	sun**glasses**
shadow clock	sun**dial**

Draw lines across the sun to connect 2 rays that add up to 92. You will draw 6 different lines, and each ray will be used only once.

Make 3 different words by adding one letter to the word SUN. Example: STUN

sunk **sung** **spun** shun

The answer is **the sun**. Write 2 questions.

1. ____
2. ____

Page 43

Sunshine

Find the hidden joke and its answer. Read the directions below and cross off words. Then read the remaining words from left to right. Write the joke and its answer on the lines.

Joke

INDIGO	POWER	WHAT	HAPPY	TERRIFIC	TON
HAPPENED	SUNSHINE	CAT	TO	CAVES	PETS
BEAR	BEAUTIFUL	SOLAR	MAUVE	THE	QUART
MAN	IGLOO	WHO	PAPER	INTO	STAYED
MADE	SUPER	POT	UP	MAGENTA	QUACK
ALL	FADED	NIGHT	TERRIBLE	ADD	BIG
QUIVER	TEAL	PLAYFUL	SALAD	WONDERING	QUIZ
WHERE	HIDE	QUEEN	HOMEWORK	TAN	THE
ABSENT	AMBER	SUN	SPIT	POLAR	TINY
BORING	REED	BOAT	WENT	?	OUTSIDE

What happened to the man who stayed up all night wondering where the sun went?

Answer

QUEST	IT	FILE	MAKEUP	FINALLY	KEYHOLE
TACKY	BEAST	DAWNED	BEIGE	WITHOUT	ON
SALES	POPCORN	HIDE	HIM	LOOP	QUIT

It finally dawned on him.

- In each row, cross off the word that comes first in alphabetical order.
- Cross off each word with the pattern: **consonant, vowel, consonant, vowel, consonant.**
- Cross off the words that are 3 letters or longer and that make other words if you write them backward.
- Cross off the names of colors.
- Cross off the adjectives beginning with B or T.
- Cross off the words with Q in them.
- Cross off the compound words.

Page 44

Snow Day!

Number the snow activities from 1 to 8 according to how much you would like to do them. The one you like the best should be number 1.

____ building a snowman
____ having a snowball fight
____ sledding
____ making snow angels
____ taking a walk in the snow
____ watching snow fall from indoors
____ skiing or snowboarding
____ building a snow fort

Marcos, Tanya, Alan, and Julia went sledding. The oldest child's sled was the fastest. The two youngest children went together on one sled. Tanya and Alan did **not** go together.

Write T if the statement is true, F if it is false, and C if you cannot tell.

T Julie and Marcos are the youngest.
C The oldest is Alan.
T Either Tanya or Alan went the fastest.
C Marcos is older than Julia.
F Tanya and Alan went together.

The answer is **a big snowball**. Write 3 different questions.

1. ____
2. ____
3. ____

SIMILES

The snow was as cold as ____
The white snow was like ____
The snowy path was as slippery as ____

Page 45

Snow Day!

If it snows three-fourths of an inch in half an hour, how many inches of snow will there be in 4 hours?
6 inches
In 7½ hours?
11¼ inches

What are 5 things besides a carrot that would make a good nose for a snowman?

1. ____
2. ____
3. ____
4. ____

You want to go out and play in the snow, but you cannot find a pair of mittens or gloves. What do you do?

____

People often put sand on the road to keep their cars from slipping on the ice and snow. Explain why this works.

____

Draw It:
There are 3 snowmen. The one on the right is the tallest. The one in the middle is the shortest. The tallest snowman is holding a shovel. The snowman on the left is the only one **not** wearing a hat. The shortest snowman is wearing a scarf. All of the snowmen are smiling.

Page 46

Snow Day!

Pretend that you are looking down on a long patch of snow from above. For each situation, draw what the prints would look like going from one end to the other.

an adult and a child walking side by side

an person and a dog

a person dragging a stick

a person pulling a sled with runners

Page 47

Name _____

Earthquakes and Volcanoes

Which would be scarier, to be caught near a volcano when it erupts or to be caught in a big earthquake? _____ Why? _____

Use the clues to find the words. The letters can all be found in *VOLCANOES*.

helps to walk	**cane**
not to win	**lose**
nearby	**close**
chilly	**cool**
caverns	**caves**
not crazy	**sane**
on your face	**nose**
not tight	**loose**
paddle in them	**canoes**

Scientists estimate that about 500,000 earthquakes occur each year on our planet. Most of these cannot be felt and very few cause damage. If there are 500,000 earthquakes in a year, about how many occur each day? Circle the correct answer.

A. more than 2,000
B. more than 1,000
C. less than 1,000
D. less than 500

Complete each sentence.

The earthquake _____ the volcano _____?

Page 48

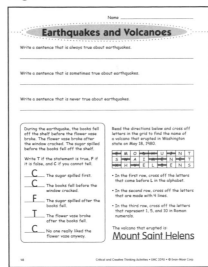

Name _____

Earthquakes and Volcanoes

Write a sentence that is always true about earthquakes. _____

Write a sentence that is sometimes true about earthquakes. _____

Write a sentence that is never true about earthquakes. _____

During the earthquake, the books fell off the shelf before the flower vase broke. The flower vase broke after the window cracked. The sugar spilled before the books fell off the shelf.

Write T if the statement is true, F if it is false, and C if you cannot tell.

C The sugar spilled first.

C The books fell before the window cracked.

F The sugar spilled after the books fell.

T The flower vase broke after the books fell.

C No one really liked the flower vase anyway.

Read the directions below and cross off letters in the grid to find the name of a volcano that erupted in Washington state on May 18, 1980.

C	M	O	U	N	T
S	A	I	N	T
H	E	L	E	N	S

• In the first row, cross off the letters that come before L in the alphabet.
• In the second row, cross off the letters that are made with 4 lines.
• In the third row, cross off the letters that represent 1, 5, and 10 in Roman numerals.

The volcano that erupted is:
Mount Saint Helens

Page 49

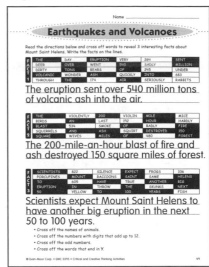

Name _____

Earthquakes and Volcanoes

Read the directions below and cross off words to reveal 3 interesting facts about Mount Saint Helens. Write the facts on the lines.

FACT 1

THE	DAY	ERUPTION	VERY	264	SENT
DEER	OVER	WENT	540	SADLY	MILLION
DIRTY	TONS	BEARS	OF	245	UNDER
VOLCANIC	WONDER	ASH	QUICKLY	INTO	683
THROUGH	THE	174	AIR	SERIOUSLY	RABBITS

The eruption sent over 540 million tons of volcanic ash into the air.

FACT 2

THE	VIOLENTLY	200	VIOLIN	MILE	MICE
BIRDS	AN	LAST	192	HOUR	HARDLY
BLAST	534	SMOKE	OF	BADLY	FIRE
SQUIRRELS	AND	ASH	SQUIRT	DESTROYED	150
SQUARE	WIVES	MILES	OF	480	FOREST

The 200-mile-an-hour blast of fire and ash destroyed 150 square miles of forest.

FACT 3

SCIENTISTS	822	SILENCE	EXPECT	FROGS	336
PORCUPINES	MOUNT	RACCOONS	SAINT	SAME	HELENS
TO	605	HAVE	TRUE	ANOTHER	BIG
ERUPTION	IN	THROW	THE	SKUNKS	NEXT
50	YELLOW	TO	100	YEARS	FISH

Scientists expect Mount Saint Helens to have another big eruption in the next 50 to 100 years.

• Cross off the names of animals.
• Cross off the numbers with digits that add up to 12.
• Cross off the odd numbers.
• Cross off the words that end in Y.

Page 50

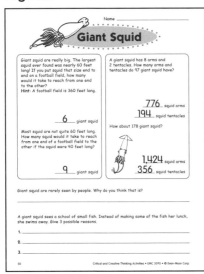

Name _____

Giant Squid

Giant squid are really big. The largest squid ever found was nearly 60 feet long! If you put squid that size end to end on a football field, how many would it take to reach from one end to the other?
Hint: A football field is 360 feet long.

6 giant squid

A giant squid has 8 arms and 2 tentacles. How many arms and tentacles do 97 giant squid have?

776 squid arms
194 squid tentacles

How about 178 giant squid?

1,424 squid arms
356 squid tentacles

Most squid are not quite 60 feet long. How many squid would it take to reach from one end of a football field to the other if the squid were 40 feet long?

9 giant squid

Giant squid are rarely seen by people. Why do you think that is? _____

A giant squid sees a school of small fish. Instead of making some of the fish her lunch, she swims away. Give 3 possible reasons.

1. _____
2. _____
3. _____

Page 51

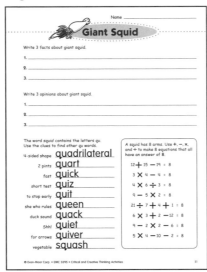

Name _____

Giant Squid

Write 3 facts about giant squid.
1. _____
2. _____
3. _____

Write 3 opinions about giant squid.
1. _____
2. _____
3. _____

The word squid contains the letters qu. Use the clues to find other qu words.

4-sided shape	**quadrilateral**
2 pints	**quart**
fast	**quick**
short test	**quiz**
to stop early	**quit**
she who rules	**queen**
duck sound	**quack**
Shh!	**quiet**
for arrows	**quiver**
vegetable	**squash**

A squid has 8 arms. Use +, −, ×, and ÷ to make 8 equations that all have an answer of 8.

12 + 15 − 19 = 8
3 × 4 − 4 = 8
4 × 6 ÷ 3 = 8
9 − 5 × 2 = 8
21 ÷ 7 + 4 + 1 = 8
6 × 3 + 2 − 12 = 8
2 − 2 × 2 − 6 = 8
5 × 4 − 10 − 2 = 8

Page 52

Name _____

Giant Squid

Each arm on this giant squid has suction cups containing numbers that make a pattern. Fill in the missing numbers to complete the number pattern on each arm.

Page 53

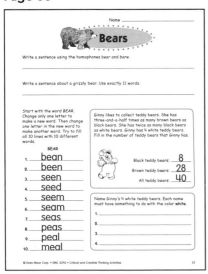

Name _____

Bears

Write a sentence using the homophones bear and bare. _____

Write a sentence about a grizzly bear. Use exactly 11 words. _____

Start with the word *BEAR*. Change only one letter to make a new word. Then change one letter in the new word to make another new word. Try to fill all 10 lines with 10 different words.

BEAR
1. **bean**
2. **been**
3. **seen**
4. **seed**
5. **seem**
6. **seam**
7. **seas**
8. **peas**
9. **peal**
10. **meal**

Ginny likes to collect teddy bears. She has three-and-a-half times as many brown bears as black bears. Ginny has twice as many black bears as white bears. Ginny has 4 white teddy bears. Fill in the number of teddy bears that Ginny has.

Black teddy bears: **8**
Brown teddy bears: **28**
All teddy bears: **40**

Name Ginny's 4 white teddy bears. Each name must have something to do with the color white.
1. _____
2. _____
3. _____
4. _____

Page 54

Name _____

Bears

What if people hibernated like bears do? Fill in the chart with 3 advantages and 3 disadvantages.

Advantages	Disadvantages

How many different kinds of bears can you name?

1. **grizzly**   3. **black**   5. **sun**
2. **polar**   4. **brown**   6. **Asian black**

Bob the Bear had an exciting day! He ate some berries after he scratched his back on a tree trunk. He wandered around the woods before he took a drink from the stream. He scratched his back on the tree after he drank from the stream. Write the 4 things Bob did in the correct order.

First: **wandered**
Second: **drank**
Third: **scratched**
Fourth: **ate berries**

Bears are omnivores and will eat almost anything. What are 6 things that you think bears eat in the wild?

1. **fish**
2. **berries**
3. **insects**
4. **grubs/worms**
5. **roots**
6. **honey**

Page 55

Name _____

Bears

Use the clues to fill in the horizontal boxes. When you are done, the vertical boxes outlined in bold will spell out the name of a constellation that looks like a bear.

1. What baby bears are called
2. Large brown bear
3. A bear's strongest sense
4. Smokey Bear is this type
5. What the bear went "over" in a song
6. Bears like to eat this large, pink-fleshed fish
7. Park where Yogi Bear lives
8. White bear
9. What bears do in winter

1. C U B S
2. G R I Z Z L Y
3. S M E L L
4. B L A C K
5. M O U N T A I N
6. S A L M O N
7. J E L L Y S T O N E
8. P O L A R
9. H I B E R N A T E

The name of a constellation that looks like a bear is **Ursa Major**

Page 56

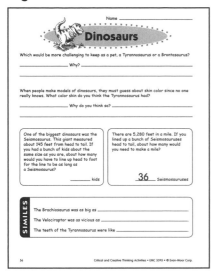

Name _____

Dinosaurs

Which would be more challenging to keep as a pet, a Tyrannosaurus or a Brontosaurus?

_____ Why? _____

When people make models of dinosaurs, they must guess about skin color since no one really knows. What color skin do you think the Tyrannosaurus had?

_____ Why do you think so? _____

One of the biggest dinosaurs was the Seismosaurus. This giant measured about 145 feet from head to tail. If you had a bunch of kids about the same size as you are, about how many would you have to line up head to foot for the line to be as long as a Seismosaurus? _____ kids	There are 5,280 feet in a mile. If you lined up a bunch of Seismosaurus head to tail, about how many would you need to make a mile? **36** Seismosauruses

SIMILES

The Brachiosaurus was as big as _____

The Velociraptor was as vicious as _____

The teeth of the Tyrannosaurus were like _____

56

Critical and Creative Thinking Activities • EMC 3395 • © Evan-Moor Corp.

Page 57

Name _____

Dinosaurs

There are many theories about why the dinosaurs became extinct. Make up a silly theory about this mystery.

The dinosaurs became extinct because _____

_____

Fill in the Venn diagram with at least 3 things in each section.

Pterodactyl — Both — Hawk

scaly skin
extinct
dinosaur

fly
have 2 legs
have wings
lay eggs

has feathers
living now
bird

Oh dear, you have accidentally entered a time portal which has sent you back to the time of the dinosaurs! Not only that, a large meat-eating dinosaur has just spotted you. What are 3 things that you can do to keep from being eaten?

1. _____
2. _____
3. _____

© Evan-Moor Corp. • EMC 3395 • Critical and Creative Thinking Activities

57

Page 58

Name _____

Dinosaurs

Dinosaurs are often given Greek or Latin names that describe them. For example, the name "Brontosaurus" means thunder (bronto) lizard (saurus). Use the chart to find out what these other dinosaur names mean.

Allosaurus	**strange lizard**	allo	strange
Velociraptor	**fast thief**	alti	tall
Deinonychus	**terrible claw**	angusti	sharp
Diceratops	**two horned head**	apato	deceptive
Monolophosaurus	**single ridged lizard**	canthus	spiked
Ornithomimus	**bird mimic**		cephalo	head
			horned
Micropachycephalosaurus		denti	round
small thick headed lizard		derm	terrible
		di	tooth
			skin

Write a dinosaur name for each description.

sharp claw	**angustinychus**	lopho	two
flat head lizard	**placocephalosaurus**	luro	ridged
winged thief	**pteroraptor**	macro	tail
pointed-tailed lizard	**mucrolurosaurus**	mega	large
thick-skinned lizard	**pachydermsaurus**	micro	large
big-toothed lizard	**macrodentisaurus**	mimus	small
		nychus	mimic
			single
			pointed
			claw
			bird
			thick
			foot
			flat
			winged

Make up a dinosaur of your own. Draw a picture of it on the back, and then name it.

raptor	thief
saurus	lizard
tops	head
tri	three
veloci	fast

58

Critical and Creative Thinking Activities • EMC 3395 • © Evan-Moor Corp.

Page 59

Name _____

Time for Dessert!

About how many desserts a week do you think a person your age should eat? _____

Why? _____

Do you think you will eat more or fewer desserts when you are an adult? _____

Why? _____

Rate the desserts from 1 to 10 according to how much you like them. The one you like the most should be number 1.

____ hot fudge sundae
____ apple pie
____ orange jello
____ chocolate cake
____ carrot cake
____ vanilla pudding
____ chocolate chip cookies
____ lemon bars
____ brownies
____ strawberry shortcake

Use the list of desserts that you rated to answer the questions below.

Would you rather have the dessert you rated number 5 every day for the next year or have the dessert you rated number 1 once a week for the next year?

_____

Which dessert would your mother choose as her favorite?

_____

How about your father?

_____

Which dessert do you think would be the hardest to make?

_____

Write a sentence about dessert. Use exactly 5 words.

_____

© Evan-Moor Corp. • EMC 3395 • Critical and Creative Thinking Activities

59

Page 60

Name _____

Time for Dessert!

Carrie's father has made her favorite dessert, but Carrie does not eat any of it. List 3 possible reasons.

1. _____
2. _____
3. _____

Name a dessert that

is creamy _____

is gooey _____

is crunchy _____

contains cinnamon _____

has nuts in it _____

smells good _____

you do not like _____

Cody has made brownies in a large rectangular pan. He wants to cut the batch into exactly 24 brownies. How many cuts will he need to make? **8** cuts

Think of a dessert. Write sentences to tell about it.

Write a sentence that is always true about the dessert.

_____

Write a sentence that is sometimes true about the dessert.

_____

Write a sentence that is never true about the dessert.

_____

60

Critical and Creative Thinking Activities • EMC 3395 • © Evan-Moor Corp.

Page 61

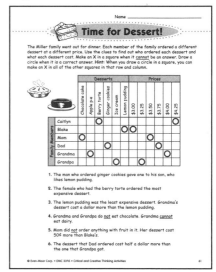

Name _____

Time for Dessert!

The Miller family went out for dinner. Each member of the family ordered a different dessert at a different price. Use the clues to find out who ordered each dessert and what each dessert cost. Make an X in a square when it cannot be an answer. Draw a circle when it is a correct answer. Hint: When you draw a circle in a square, you can make an X in all of the other squares in that row and column.

		Desserts						Prices				
		Chocolate cake	Apple pie	Berry torte	Ginger cookies	Ice cream	Lemon pudding	$3.00	$3.25	$3.50	$3.75	$4.00	$4.25
Family Members	Caitlyn												
	Blake				O								
	Mom	O							O				
	Dad						O						
	Grandma												
	Grandpa	O											

1. The man who ordered ginger cookies gave one to his son, who likes lemon pudding.
2. The female who had the berry torte ordered the most expensive dessert.
3. The lemon pudding was the least expensive dessert. Grandma's dessert cost a dollar more than the lemon pudding.
4. Grandma and Grandpa do not eat chocolate. Grandma cannot eat dairy.
5. Mom did not order anything with fruit in it. Her dessert cost 50¢ more than Blake's.
6. The dessert that Dad ordered cost half a dollar more than the one that Grandpa got.

© Evan-Moor Corp. • EMC 3395 • Critical and Creative Thinking Activities

61

Page 62

Name _____

Pizza

Explain a pizza to someone who has never seen or tasted one.

What is Lorenzo's favorite pizza topping? Follow the directions and rewrite the word on each new line until you find out.

	L O R E N Z O
Change the fourth letter to the letter that comes just before T in the alphabet.	L O R S N Z O
Change the first O to the vowel that is in both LAUGHTER and SAILING.	L A R S N Z O
Change the second O to the vowel that is in both EATING and CUTE.	L A R S N Z E
Make the fifth letter the same as the second letter.	L A R S A Z E
Change the first letter to the letter that is used most often to make a singular word plural.	S A R S A Z E
Change the second-to-the-last letter to the seventh letter in the alphabet.	S A R S A G E
Change the third letter to the letter that comes three letters after it in the alphabet.	S A U S A G E

What is your favorite pizza topping? _____

The answer is a pepperoni pizza. Write 3 different questions.

1. _____
2. _____
3. _____

62

Critical and Creative Thinking Activities • EMC 3395 • © Evan-Moor Corp.

Page 63

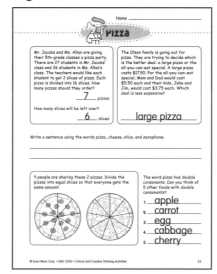

Name _____

Pizza

Mr. Jacobs and Ms. Allan are giving their 5th-grade classes a pizza party. There are 27 students in Mr. Jacobs' class and 26 students in Ms. Allan's class. The teachers would like each student to get 2 slices of pizza. Each pizza is divided in 16 slices. How many pizzas should they order? **7** pizzas	The Olson family is going out for pizza. They are trying to decide which is the better deal: a large pizza or the all-you-can-eat special. A large pizza costs $17.50. For the all-you-can-eat special, Mom and Dad would cost $5.50 each and their kids, Jake and Jim, would cost $3.75 each. Which deal is less expensive? **large pizza**

How many slices will be left over? **6** slices

Write a sentence using the words pizza, cheese, slice, and saxophone.

_____

9 people are sharing these 2 pizzas. Divide the pizzas into equal slices so that everyone gets the same amount.

The word pizza has double consonants. Can you think of 5 other foods with double consonants?

1. **apple**
2. **carrot**
3. **egg**
4. **cabbage**
5. **cherry**

© Evan-Moor Corp. • EMC 3395 • Critical and Creative Thinking Activities

63

Page 64

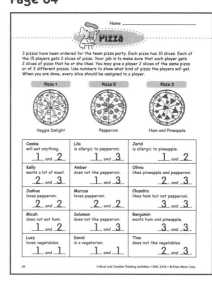

Name _____

Pizza

3 pizzas have been ordered for the team pizza party. Each pizza has 10 slices. Each of the 15 players gets 2 slices of pizza. Your job is to make sure that each player gets 2 slices of pizza that he or she likes. You may give a player 2 slices of the same pizza or of 2 different pizzas. Use numbers to show what kind of pizza the players will get. When you are done, every slice should be assigned to a player.

Pizza 1 — Veggie Delight
Pizza 2 — Pepperoni
Pizza 3 — Ham and Pineapple

Cassie will eat anything. **1** and **2**	**Lila** is allergic to pepperoni. **1** and **3**	**Jarid** is allergic to pineapple. **1** and **2**
Kelly wants a lot of meat. **2** and **3**	**Amber** does not like pepperoni. **1** and **3**	**Olivia** likes pineapple and pepperoni. **2** and **3**
Joshua loves pepperoni. **2** and **2**	**Marcus** loves pepperoni. **2** and **2**	**Chandra** likes ham but not pepperoni. **3** and **3**
Micah does not eat ham. **1** and **2**	**Solomon** does not like pepperoni. **1** and **3**	**Benjamin** wants ham and pineapple. **3** and **3**
Lucy loves vegetables. **1** and **1**	**David** is a vegetarian. **1** and **1**	**Tina** does not like vegetables. **2** and **3**

64

Critical and Creative Thinking Activities • EMC 3395 • © Evan-Moor Corp.

© Evan-Moor Corp. • EMC 3395 • Critical and Creative Thinking Activities

149

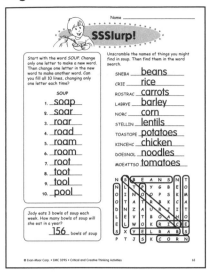

SSSlurp!

Start with the word *SOUP*. Change only one letter to make a new word. Then change one letter in the new word to make another word. Can you fill all 10 lines, changing only one letter each time?

SOUP
1. soap
2. soar
3. roar
4. road
5. roam
6. room
7. root
8. toot
9. tool
10. pool

Unscramble the names of things you might find in soup. Then find them in the word search.

SNEBA — beans
CRIE — rice
ROSTRAC — carrots
LABRYE — barley
NORC — corn
STELLIN — lentils
TOASTOPE — potatoes
KINCEHC — chicken
DOESNOL — noodles
MOEATTSO — tomatoes

Jody eats 3 bowls of soup each week. How many bowls of soup will she eat in a year?
156 bowls of soup

SSSlurp!

How many different kinds of soup can you name?

Circle the letter of the correct statement to complete each syllogism.

All carrots are vegetables.
Some soups have carrots.
Therefore,
A. all soups have vegetables
B. some soups have vegetables
C. all vegetables are carrots

Everything homemade is yummy.
Some soups are homemade.
Therefore,
A. some soups are yummy
B. all soups are yummy
C. some soups are salads

Here is a bowl of alphabet soup. Use the back if you need to.

Possible answers include:
1. cake
2. make
3. take
4. wake
5. rake
6. meat
7. heat
8. great
9. wheat
10. greet
11. clean
12. lean
13. learn
14. wheel
15. calm
16. game

SSSlurp!

It's time to make soup, but you have a double challenge. You must decide what to put in the soup to make it yummy, and you must also make sure that the points are correct. Good luck and happy cooking!

Ingredient	Points
Carrots	5 each
Celery	6 each
Onions	7 each
Potatoes	8 each
Corn	9 per cup
Lentils	10 per cup
Black beans	11 per cup
Noodles	12 per cup
Barley	13 per cup
Rice	14 per cup
Chicken	20
Beef	30
Spices	50

Make a soup that is between 100 and 120 points.

Ingredient	Amount	Points

Total Points:

Make a soup that is between 125 and 150 points.

Ingredient	Amount	Points

Total Points:

Make a soup that is between 155 and 200 points.

Ingredient	Amount	Points

Total Points:

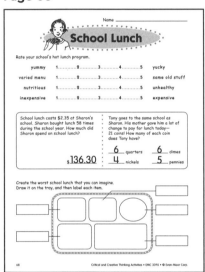

School Lunch

Rate your school's hot lunch program.

yummy 1 2 3 4 5 yucky
varied menu 1 2 3 4 5 same old stuff
nutritious 1 2 3 4 5 unhealthy
inexpensive 1 2 3 4 5 expensive

School lunch costs $2.35 at Sharon's school. Sharon bought lunch 58 times during the school year. How much did Sharon spend on school lunch?
$136.30

Tony goes to the same school as Sharon. His mother gave him a lot of change to pay for lunch today—21 coins! How many of each coin does Tony have?
6 quarters   6 dimes
4 nickels   5 pennies

Create the worst school lunch that you can imagine. Draw it on the tray, and then label each item.

School Lunch

Do you like buying school lunch?
Why or why not?

Today, there are two main-dish choices for hot lunch: pizza and a sub sandwich. For fruit, students may choose an apple or an orange. For dessert, there is a cookie or a cupcake. For a beverage, there is chocolate milk or plain milk. How many different combinations of main dish, fruit, dessert, and beverage are there?
16 different combinations

Which would you choose for each one?
Main dish:
Fruit:
Dessert:
Beverage:

Many kids who pack their lunches bring sandwiches. How many different kinds of sandwiches can you name?
1.
2.
3.
4.
5.
6.
7.
8.
9.
10.
Draw a ★ next to the one you like the most. Make an X next to the ones you do not like.

SIMILES
The meatball was as hard as
The pizza was as greasy
The rubbery meat was like

School Lunch

All of the children listed below are very picky about the lunches they eat at school. Each of the items in each child's lunch must start with the same letter as his or her name. Fill in the chart to make each child a lunch.

Name	Main Dish	Fruit or Veggie	Snack or Dessert	Drink
Sarah				
Pete				
Carlos				
Trina				
Michael				
Fiona				
Gina				

Garrett and Jennifer both have double letters in their names. Can you make two different lunches that both have foods with double letters?

Name	Main Dish	Fruit or Veggie	Snack or Dessert	Drink
Garrett				
Jennifer				

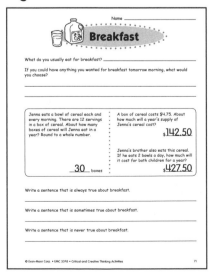

Breakfast

What do you usually eat for breakfast?

If you could have anything you wanted for breakfast tomorrow morning, what would you choose?

Jenna eats a bowl of cereal each and every morning. There are 12 servings in a box of cereal. About how many boxes of cereal will Jenna eat in a year? Round to a whole number.
30 boxes

A box of cereal costs $4.75. About how much will a year's supply of Jenna's cereal cost?
$142.50

Jenna's brother also eats this cereal. If he eats 2 bowls a day, how much will it cost for both children for a year?
$427.50

Write a sentence that is always true about breakfast.

Write a sentence that is sometimes true about breakfast.

Write a sentence that is never true about breakfast.

Breakfast

Many people believe that breakfast is the most important meal of the day. Why do you think this is?

Kit has made a yummy bowl of oatmeal. She added milk to her oatmeal before she added raisins. She added almonds after the milk. She added brown sugar before the raisins.

Write T if the statement is true, F if it is false, and C if you cannot tell.

F Kit added raisins after the milk.
C Kit added almonds before the brown sugar.
C Kit added milk before the brown sugar.
C Kit added raisins and almonds at the same time.
T Kit added raisins after the brown sugar.
C Kit likes oatmeal.

How many different breakfast foods can you think of?
1.
2.
3.
4.
5.
6.
7.
8.
9.
10.

Complete the sentences.
_____ pancakes and maple syrup _____
_____ for breakfast?
Eggs are not _____

Breakfast

Solve the breakfast crossword puzzle ... don't eat it!

JUICE / EGG / SYRUP / YOGURT / MUFFIN / DOUGHNUT / PANCAKES / BACON / CEREAL / JELLY / MAPLE / MILK / MORNING / BANANA / TOAST / SPOON / BAGEL

ACROSS
1. Breakfast drink
5. Good on cereal
8. Good on pancakes
9. Plain or fruit-flavored milk product
11. Fruit with a yellow peel
13. Blueberry or bran
14. Use to eat cereal
15. Glazed with a hole
17. In a stack with syrup
19. Breakfast meat in strips
20. Fruit spread
21. Kind of syrup

DOWN
2. Scramble or fry them
3. Yellow part of an egg
4. Breakfast time
6. 3 bears' food
7. For flipping pancakes
8. Heated bread
10. Dried grapes
12. Holds your oatmeal
16. A cooked cereal
18. Good with cream cheese

Page 74

Play Ball!

Name _____

Write 3 ways that the game of baseball would change if the ball were cube-shaped.

1. _____
2. _____

Write 3 ways that the game of baseball would change if it were played in a swamp.

1. _____
2. _____
3. _____

SIMILES

The pitch was as fast as _____
The crack of the bat was like _____
The cheering of the crowd was like _____

How are basketball and baseball the same and different? Write 3 ways for each.

Same	Different

Page 75

Play Ball!

Name _____

Would you rather be the best player on a losing team or the worst player on a winning team?

_____ Why? _____

Would you rather play all your games in perfect weather but lose all of them, or would you rather win every game but always have to play in the rain?

_____ Why? _____

"It's not whether you win or lose, it's how you play the game."

Do you agree with this saying? _____

Why or why not? _____

Amber, Carly, Rachel, and Zoe all play on the same softball team. Read the clues to find out who plays each position.

• Zoe is not the pitcher or the shortstop.
• Rachel, who is not the catcher, did not throw the ball to Carly or Zoe when she helped to get a batter out at first base.
• Carly is best friends with the shortstop.

First base: Amber
Pitcher: Carly
Catcher: Zoe
Shortstop: Rachel

Write a sentence using the words *baseball, bat, hit,* and *hippopotamus.*

Page 76

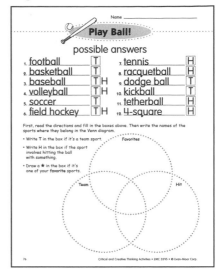

Play Ball!

Name _____

possible answers

1. football	T		7. tennis	H	
2. basketball	T		8. racquetball	H	
3. baseball	T H		9. dodge ball	T	
4. volleyball	T H		10. kickball	T	
5. soccer	T		11. tetherball	H	
6. field hockey	T H		12. 4-square	H	

First, read the directions and fill in the boxes above. Then write the names of the sports where they belong in the Venn diagram.

• Write T in the box if it's a team sport.
• Write H in the box if the sport involves hitting the ball with something.
• Draw a ★ in the box if it's one of your favorite sports.

Favorites

Team

Hit

Page 77

It's All About Speed

Name _____

In some sports, it is important to be able to go fast. Name as many of those sports as you can.

1. ____ 4. ____ 7. ____
2. ____ 5. ____ 8. ____
3. ____ 6. ____ 9. ____

Circle the letter of the statement that completes each syllogism.

Some people are runners.
All runners are fast.
Therefore, ____

A. some runners are people
B. some people are fast
C. all people are fast

Some women like pizza.
Some skiers are women.
Therefore, ____

A. all skiers like pizza
B. no skiers like pizza
C. some skiers like pizza

Read the statements below, and then fill in the chart to show the miles each person can run in the number of minutes shown. Reduce the fractions.

• Janet can run a mile in 6 minutes.
• Jack can run a mile in 8 minutes.
• Chrissy can run a mile in 10 minutes.

Minutes	Janet	Jack	Chrissy
4 minutes	$\frac{2}{3}$	$\frac{1}{2}$	$\frac{2}{5}$
12 minutes	2	$1\frac{1}{2}$	$1\frac{1}{5}$
18 minutes	3	$2\frac{1}{4}$	$1\frac{4}{5}$
20 minutes	$3\frac{1}{3}$	$2\frac{1}{2}$	2
24 minutes	4	3	$2\frac{2}{5}$

Page 78

It's All About Speed

Name _____

Which of these kinds of races would you most like to be in: ski, horse, or bike?

_____ Why? _____

Which of those kinds of races do you think is the most dangerous?

_____ Why? _____

Besides a car, what is the fastest thing you have ever ridden on or in?

Number the activities from 1 to 4 according to how fast you can do them. The one you can do the fastest should be number 1.

____ skating
____ swimming
____ running
____ biking

Four girls had a race. Blair was faster than Natalie. Natalie was faster than Jo. Jo was slower than Blair. Tootie was faster than Blair. In what order did the girls finish the race?

First: Tootie
Second: Blair
Third: Natalie
Fourth: Jo

What does it mean to "jump the gun" in a race?

What does it mean to "jump the gun" in a situation that is not a race?

Use the expression "jump the gun" in a sentence.

Page 79

It's All About Speed

Name _____

The 5 children listed below all ride their bikes to school. Fill in the chart to show each child's average speed. Then use the chart to answer the questions.
Hint: *mph* means *miles per hour.*

	Monday	Tuesday	Wednesday	Thursday	Friday	Average
Chris	11 mph	12 mph	14 mph	16 mph	12 mph	13
Tracy	11 mph	10 mph	13 mph	14 mph	12 mph	12
Danny	15 mph	13 mph	16 mph	17 mph	14 mph	15
Laurie	17 mph	15 mph	16 mph	19 mph	18 mph	17
Keith	19 mph	17 mph	18 mph	17 mph	19 mph	18

Which child had the fastest speed on Thursday? Laurie
Which child had the fastest speed on Monday? Keith
Which child had the fastest average speed? Keith
What is the average speed of all 5 children? 15 mph

The school is 4 miles from Danny's house. How long did it take him to get to school on Wednesday? 15 minutes

Keith lives 3 miles from the school. How long did it take him to ride to school on Monday? 10 minutes

What are 3 possible reasons why Keith rides faster than Chris?

1. _____
2. _____
3. _____

Page 80

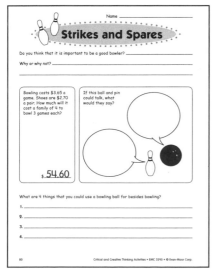

Strikes and Spares

Name _____

Do you think that it is important to be a good bowler? _____

Why or why not? _____

Bowling costs $3.65 a game. Shoes are $2.70 a pair. How much will it cost a family of 4 to bowl 3 games each?

$54.60

If this ball and pin could talk, what would they say?

What are 4 things that you could use a bowling ball for besides bowling?

1. _____
2. _____
3. _____
4. _____

Page 81

Strikes and Spares

Name _____

Write a sentence about bowling. Use exactly 10 words.

Write a sentence using the words *ball, strike, pins,* and *spaghetti.*

Use the clues to find words that rhyme with either *BALL* or *PIN.*

holds the ceiling up wall
holds your insides in skin
season fall
not short tall
to turn around and around spin
on a fish fin
to use a phone call
on your face chin
many stores together mall

Shaun went bowling today. Use the clues to find out what his score was.

• Shaun's score was more than 100 but less than 135.
• The sum of the tens and the ones digits is 7.
• The score is not odd.
• The tens and the ones digits are consecutive.

Shaun's score: 134

Compose a short rhyming poem about bowling. Use the words *pin* and *win.*

Page 82

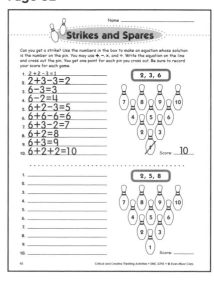

Strikes and Spares

Name _____

Can you get a strike? Use the numbers in the box to make an equation whose solution is the number on the pin. You may use +, −, ×, and ÷. Write the equation on the line and cross out the pin. You get one point for each pin you cross out. Be sure to record your score for each game.

2, 3, 6

1. $2 + 2 - 3 = 1$
2. $2 + 3 - 3 = 2$
3. $6 - 3 = 3$
4. $6 - 2 = 4$
5. $6 + 2 - 3 = 5$
6. $6 + 6 - 6 = 6$
7. $6 + 3 - 2 = 7$
8. $6 + 2 = 8$
9. $6 + 3 = 9$
10. $6 + 2 + 2 = 10$

Score: 10

2, 5, 8

1. _____
2. _____
3. _____
4. _____
5. _____
6. _____
7. _____
8. _____
9. _____
10. _____

Score: ____

Page 83

Page 84

Page 85

Page 86

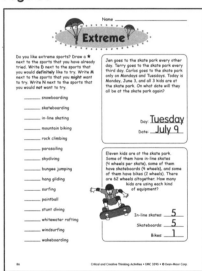

Page 87

Page 88

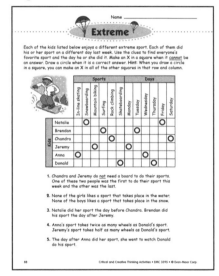

Page 89

Page 90

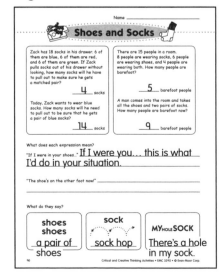

Page 91

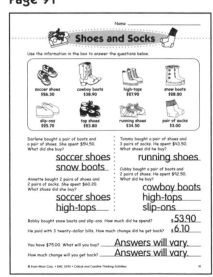

Page 92

Spoons and Forks

If you could use only a spoon or a fork for the rest of your life, which would you choose?

Why? _____

What are 5 things that you could use a spoon or fork for besides eating?

Spoon	Fork
1.	1.
2.	2.
3.	3.
4.	4.
5.	5.

Use the clues to find words that rhyme with either *SPOON* or *FORK*.

in the night sky	moon
ham or bacon	pork
lunchtime	noon
bottle stopper	cork
in a little while	soon
spun by a caterpillar	cocoon

Myron is in charge of buying forks for the schoolwide spaghetti feed. He bought 8 cartons of plastic forks. Each carton contains 12 boxes. Each box contains 72 forks. How many plastic forks did Myron buy?

6,912 plastic forks

Page 93

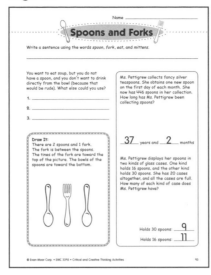

Spoons and Forks

Write a sentence using the words *spoon, fork, eat,* and *mittens.*

You want to eat soup, but you do not have a spoon, and you don't want to drink directly from the bowl (because that would be rude). What else could you use?

1. _____
2. _____
3. _____

Draw It:
There are 2 spoons and 1 fork. The fork is between the spoons. The tines of the fork are toward the top of the picture. The bowls of the spoons are toward the bottom.

Ms. Pettigrew collects fancy silver teaspoons. She obtains one new spoon on the first day of each month. She now has 446 spoons in her collection. How long has Ms. Pettigrew been collecting spoons?

37 years and **2** months

Ms. Pettigrew displays her spoons in two kinds of glass cases. One kind holds 16 spoons, and the other kind holds 30 spoons. She has 20 cases altogether, and all the cases are full. How many of each kind of case does Ms. Pettigrew have?

| Holds 30 spoons: | 9 |
| Holds 16 spoons: | 11 |

Page 94

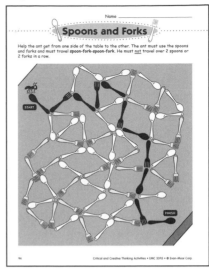

Spoons and Forks

Help the ant get from one side of the table to the other. The ant must use the spoons and forks and must travel **spoon-fork-spoon-fork**. He must <u>not</u> travel over 2 spoons or 2 forks in a row.

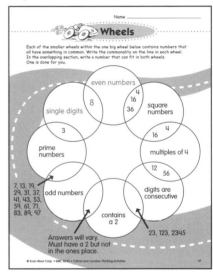

Page 95

Wheels

The answer is **It had big wheels.** What is the question?

_____

Unscramble the things that have wheels, and then write the words in the grid.

ARC	car
TRAC	cart
KRUCT	truck
NARIT	train
GONAW	wagon
STESKA	skates
CROTES	scooter
LYCEBIC	bicycle
RICCETLY	tricycle
CRATTOR	tractor
TORKDABASE	skateboard
CROEMCOTLY	motorcycle
HERLCAHEWI	wheelchair

Why do you think that most cars have 4 wheels instead of 3 or 5?

Page 96

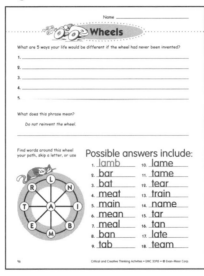

Wheels

What are 5 ways your life would be different if the wheel had never been invented?

1. _____
2. _____
3. _____
4. _____
5. _____

What does this phrase mean?

Do not reinvent the wheel.

Find words around this wheel your path, skip a letter, or use

Possible answers include:

1. lamb
2. bar
3. bat
4. meat
5. main
6. mean
7. meal
8. ban
9. tab
10. lame
11. tame
12. tear
13. train
14. name
15. tar
16. tan
17. late
18. team

Page 97

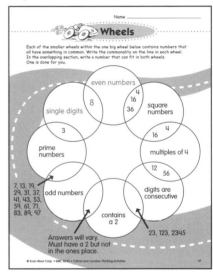

Wheels

Each of the smaller wheels within the one big wheel below contains numbers that all have something in common. Write the commonality on the line in each wheel. In the overlapping section, write a number that can fit in both wheels. One is done for you.

even numbers — 8, 4, 16, 36
single digits — 3
square numbers
prime numbers — 7, 13, 19, 29, 31, 37, 41, 43, 53, 59, 61, 71, 83, 89, 97
multiples of 4 — 4, 16
odd numbers
contains a 2 — 12, 56
digits are consecutive — 23, 123, 2345

Answers will vary. Must have a 2 but not in the ones place.

Page 98

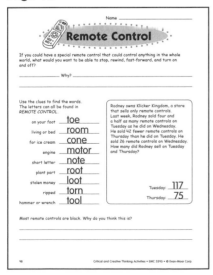

Remote Control

If you could have a special remote control that could control anything in the whole world, what would you want to be able to stop, rewind, fast-forward, and turn on and off?

Why? _____

Use the clues to find the words. The letters can all be found in *REMOTE CONTROL.*

on your foot	toe
living or bed	room
for ice cream	cone
engine	motor
short letter	note
plant part	root
stolen money	loot
ripped	torn
hammer or wrench	tool

Rodney owns Klicker Kingdom, a store that sells only remote controls. Last week, Rodney sold four and a half as many remote controls on Tuesday as he did on Wednesday. He sold 42 fewer remote controls on Thursday than he did on Tuesday. He sold 26 remote controls on Wednesday. How many did Rodney sell on Tuesday and Thursday?

Tuesday: **117**
Thursday: **75**

Most remote controls are black. Why do you think this is?

Page 99

Remote Control

How do you think remote controls work?

_____

The answer is **the remote control.** What are 3 questions?

1. _____
2. _____
3. _____

How many buttons are on Tony's new remote control? Read the clues to find out.

- The number of buttons is a prime number under 50.
- The sum of the digits is 10.
- The ones digit is 4 more than the tens digit.

There are **37** buttons.

List 4 things that can have remote controls besides TVs.

1. stereo
2. DVD player
3. CD player
4. radio controlled car

You have decided to play a joke on your family by hiding the TV remote. Where would you hide it if you wanted them to...

find it quickly? _____

search for a while? _____

search all day? _____

Page 100

Remote Control

The word *remote* has an *r* and then a *t* in it. How many other words can you make that have both of those letters? The *r* <u>must</u> come before the *t*. Examples: *rate, bright*

r and t

Answers will vary. Accept any correctly spelled word that follows the rules.

3.	10.	17.	24.
4.	11.	18.	25.
5.	12.	19.	26.
6.	13.	20.	27.
7.	14.	21.	28.

Now try *c* and *l,* like in the word *control.*

c and l

1.	8.	15.	22.
2.	9.	16.	23.
3.	10.	17.	24.
4.	11.	18.	25.
5.	12.	19.	26.
6.	13.	20.	27.
7.	14.	21.	28.

Page 101

Money

How much money do you think a person has to have to be rich?

Underline one for each choice. Would you rather...

be smart or be rich?

have $500 right now or have $1,000 in a year?

get $100 every day for the rest of your life or get one million dollars right now?

be given $1,000 or have $10,000 given to the charity of your choice?

be poor and have a loving family or be rich and live alone?

It has been said that money can't buy happiness. What are 4 other things that money can't buy?

1. _____
2. _____
3. _____
4. _____

Minimum wage is the least amount of money that an adult can be paid per hour for doing a job. How much do you think minimum wage should be? _____ Why? _____

An American dollar bill is 6 inches long. A football field is 360 feet long. How many one-dollar bills would you have to line up end to end to reach from one end of a football field to the other?

720 dollar bills

How much money would you have if they were twenty-dollar bills?

$14,400

Page 102

Money

What does each expression about money mean?

"I feel like a million bucks."

I feel terrific.

"Put your money where your mouth is."

Show you stand behind what you're saying.

"Money doesn't grow on trees."

Money isn't easily had.

What would happen if money really did grow on trees? _____

Jolene has 3 times as many five-dollar bills as she does twenty-dollar bills. She has twice as many one-dollar bills as she does five-dollar bills. She has two fewer ten-dollar bills than five-dollar bills. She also has $3.57 in change. Jolene has two twenty-dollar bills. How much money does Jolene have altogether?

$125.57

The U.S. Treasury is going to let you decide whose picture should appear on coins and bills. Write your choice for each one.

penny _____
nickel _____
dime _____
quarter _____
one-dollar bill _____
five-dollar bill _____
ten-dollar bill _____
twenty-dollar bill _____

Page 103

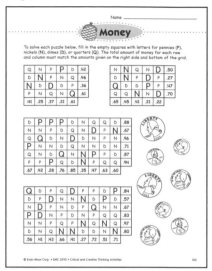

Money

To solve each puzzle below, fill in the empty squares with letters for pennies (P), nickels (N), dimes (D), or quarters (Q). The total amount of money for each row and column must match the amounts given on the right side and bottom of the grid.

Q	N	P	D	.42
D	N	P	N	.46
N	D	D	P	.36
P	N	Q	N	.61
.41	.25	.37	.21	

N	N	Q	N	D	.50
D	N	P	D	P	.27
Q	N	N	D	P	.47
Q	Q	N	N	D	.70
.65	.45	.41	.21	.22	

D	P	P	P	D	N	Q	D	.88
N	N	P	D	Q	N	D	N	.67
Q	D	N	D	Q	N	N	P	.96
Q	N	D	Q	N	N	D	N	.71
P	P	P	Q	D	N	P	Q	.94
.67	.42	.28	.76	.85	.35	.47	.63	.60

Q	D	Q	D	P	P	D	P	.84
D	P	D	N	N	N	P	D	.57
N	D	P	N	P	Q	N	N	.67
P	D	N	P	D	N	P	Q	.83
N	N	P	N	P	N	Q	Q	.97
D	N	Q	N	N	D	D	N	.80
.56	.41	.43	.66	.41	.27	.72	.51	.71

Page 104

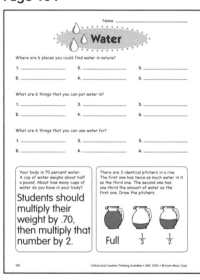

Water

Where are 6 places you could find water in nature?

1. _____ 3. _____ 5. _____
2. _____ 4. _____ 6. _____

What are 6 things that you can put water in?

1. _____ 3. _____ 5. _____
2. _____ 4. _____ 6. _____

What are 6 things that you can use water for?

1. _____ 3. _____ 5. _____
2. _____ 4. _____ 6. _____

Your body is 70 percent water. A cup of water weighs about half a pound. About how many cups of water do you have in your body?

Students should multiply their weight by .70, then multiply that number by 2.

There are 3 identical pitchers in a row. The first one has twice as much water in it as the third one. The second one has one-third the amount of water as the first one. Draw the pitchers.

Full   **⅓**   **½**

Page 105

Water

It is always a good idea to conserve water. What are 3 things that you can do to use less water?

1. _____
2. _____
3. _____

About how much water do you think it would take to fill...

your shoe? _____
your desk? _____
the wastepaper bin? _____
your classroom? _____

You have 3 cups. Cup A is 1/4 full and can hold twice as much water as cup B. Cup B is full. Cup C is the same size as cup A and is empty. If the water from cups A and B was poured into cup C, how full would cup C be?

¾ full

You have 3 pitchers. Two will hold 5 cups of water each. One will hold 7 cups of water. You need exactly 4 cups of water. Describe how you can get exactly 4 cups. You may not fill a pitcher part way and just guess the amount.

Fill up the 7-cup pitcher and use it to fill one of the 5-cup pitchers. You now have 2 cups in the 7-cup pitcher. Dump out the water from the 5-cup pitcher and put the 2 cups of water from the 7-cup pitcher in it. Fill the 7-cup pitcher with water again and use it to fill the other 5-cup pitcher. You now have 2 cups in the 7-cup pitcher. Pour those 2 cups into the 5-cup pitcher that already has 2 cups of water in it, and that leaves you with 4 cups of water.

Page 106

Water

Read the directions below and cross off words and numbers to find 3 facts about the world's largest lake. Write the facts on the lines.

THE	EXIT	51	EAR	FATE	LAKE
EXACT	IN	DEER	4,687	THE	WORLD	RICE
IS	BAFFLE	LAKE	BAIKAL	STATE	CAKE	WHICH
LITTLE	IS	LETTUCE	LOCATED	TOAST	679	HAT
EXPERT	GREAT	IN	BACK	TAX	SIBERIA	BOX

The largest lake in the world is Lake Baikal, which is located in Siberia.

LAKE	ANGLE	BAIKAL	BAIT	IS	685	MANGO
FIX	5,370	CAN	FEET	CARROT	MIXER	DEEP
PRETZEL	WEIGHT	AND	SMALL	HOLDS	AID	70
PERCENT	MINI	DARE	OF	THE	DATE
EGGS	WORLD'S	EAGLES	SURFACE	TINY	FRESH	WATER

Lake Baikal is 5,370 feet deep and holds 20 percent of the world's surface fresh water.

THERE	ARE	APPLE	EXTRA	OVER	ALL	1,700
BEAR	827	DIFFERENT	EXCEL	BITSY	SPECIES	PIZZA
OF	ACE	EXTEND	PLANTS	CORN	FREIGHT	AND
SLATE	ANIMALS	PETITE	WAIT	IN	23	ABOUT
LAKE	PEAS	BAD	BAIKAL	85	SIX	PLATE

There are over 1,700 different species of plants and animals in Lake Baikal.

- Cross off the words that have an X in them.
- Cross off the words that mean the opposite of big.
- Cross off the names of foods.
- Cross off the odd numbers.
- Cross off the words that rhyme with late.

Page 107

Light and Dark

How many different things can you think of that give off light?

1. _____ 4. _____ 7. _____
2. _____ 5. _____ 8. _____
3. _____ 6. _____ 9. _____

What are shadows? _____

Use the clues to find the words. The letters can all be found in LIGHT and DARK.

Scottish skirt **kilt**
difficult **hard**
happy **glad**
ice from the sky **hail**
throw at a target **dart**
to speak **talk**
base of a sword **hilt**
a bunny has a fluffy one **tail**
number 3 in line **third**

Emilio has 27 light bulbs in his house. It costs him 4¢ in electricity for every hour that one bulb burns. If Emilio turns on every light in his house for 12 hours, how much will it cost him in electricity?

$12.96

Page 108

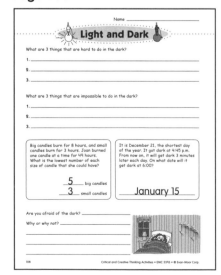

Light and Dark

What are 3 things that are hard to do in the dark?

1. _____
2. _____
3. _____

What are 3 things that are impossible to do in the dark?

1. _____
2. _____
3. _____

Big candles burn for 8 hours, and small candles burn for 3 hours. Joan burned one candle at a time for 49 hours. What is the lowest number of each size of candle that she could have?

5 big candles
3 small candles

It is December 21, the shortest day of the year. It got dark at 4:45 p.m. From now on, it will get dark 3 minutes later each day. On what date will it get dark at 6:00?

January 15

Are you afraid of the dark? _____ Why or why not? _____

Page 109

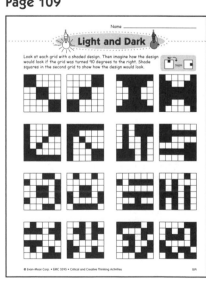

Light and Dark

Look at each grid with a shaded design. Then imagine how the design would look if the grid was turned 90 degrees to the right. Shade squares in the second grid to show how the design would look.

Page 110

Collections

Many people enjoy collecting things like shells or baseball cards. What are some other things that people collect?

1. _____ 4. _____ 7. _____
2. _____ 5. _____ 8. _____
3. _____ 6. _____ 9. _____

Why do you think people enjoy collecting things? _____
_____

Mark collects polished rocks. He has less than 35 of them. If he puts all of his rocks in two groups, there will be one left over. If he puts them in groups of three, there will be two left over. If he puts them in groups of four, there will be three left over. How many polished rocks are in Mark's collection?

23 polished rocks

Sylvia collects marbles. The number of marbles she has is 3 digits. The digits are all consecutive, and if you add them, the sum will be 15. How many marbles does Sylvia have?

456 marbles

A distant relative has left you his very valuable coin collection. What do you do with it?

_____

Why? _____

Page 111

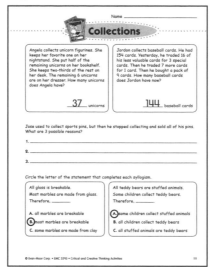

Collections

Angela collects unicorn figurines. She keeps her favorite one on her nightstand. She put half of the remaining unicorns on her bookshelf. She keeps two-thirds of the rest on her desk. The remaining 6 unicorns are on her dresser. How many unicorns does Angela have?

37 unicorns

Jordon collects baseball cards. He had 154 cards. Yesterday, he traded 16 of his less valuable cards for 3 special cards. Then he traded 7 more cards for 1 card. Then he bought a pack of 9 cards. How many baseball cards does Jordon have now?

144 baseball cards

Jose used to collect sports pins, but then he stopped collecting and sold all of his pins. What are 3 possible reasons?

1. _____
2. _____
3. _____

Circle the letter of the statement that completes each syllogism.

All glass is breakable.
Most marbles are made from glass.
Therefore,

A. all marbles are breakable
B. most marbles are breakable (circled)
C. some marbles are made from clay

All teddy bears are stuffed animals.
Some children collect teddy bears.
Therefore,

A. some children collect stuffed animals (circled)
B. all children collect teddy bears
C. all stuffed animals are teddy bears

Page 112

Collections

Many people collect state quarters. The quarters were issued in the order that each state was admitted to the Union. Color the states on the map below to show when each quarter was minted.

1999—Blue	2000—Yellow	2001—Light green	2002—Red	2003—Purple
Delaware	Massachusetts	New York	Tennessee	Illinois
Pennsylvania	Maryland	North Carolina	Ohio	Alabama
New Jersey	South Carolina	Rhode Island	Louisiana	Maine
Georgia	New Hampshire	Vermont	Indiana	Missouri
Connecticut	Virginia	Kentucky	Mississippi	Arkansas

2004—Brown	2005—Pink	2006—Light blue	2007—Green	2008—Orange
Michigan	California	Nevada	Montana	Oklahoma
Florida	Minnesota	Nebraska	Washington	New Mexico
Texas	Oregon	Colorado	Idaho	Arizona
Iowa	Kansas	North Dakota	Wyoming	Alaska
Wisconsin	West Virginia	South Dakota	Utah	Hawaii

If you had one quarter from each state, how much money would you have? $ **12.50**

Page 113

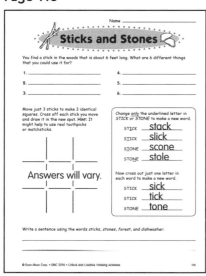

Sticks and Stones

You find a stick in the woods that is about 6 feet long. What are 6 different things that you could use it for?

1. _____ 4. _____
2. _____ 5. _____
3. _____ 6. _____

Move just 3 sticks to make 3 identical squares. Cross off each stick you move and draw it in the new spot. Hint: It might help to use real toothpicks or matchsticks.

Answers will vary.

Change only the underlined letter in STICK or STONE to make a new word.

STICK — **stack**
STICK — **slick**
STONE — **scone**
STONE — **stole**

Now cross out just one letter in each word to make a new word.

STICK — **sick**
STICK — **tick**
STONE — **tone**

Write a sentence using the words sticks, stones, forest, and dishwasher.

_____

Page 114

Sticks and Stones

"Sticks and stones may break my bones, but words will never hurt me."

Do you think this is a true statement?

Why do you think so? _____
_____

Use the clues to find other words that begin with st, like sticks and stones.

tale	**story**
to get ready for a test	**study**
smelly	**stinky**
church tower	**steeple**
to trip and fall	**stumble**
very hungry	**starving**
pupil	**student**
artist's work space	**studio**
horse's home	**stable**
strong, hard metal	**steel**
for trains or buses	**station**
make free of germs	**sterilize**

There are 3 different sizes of stones. Fill in the number of medium-sized stones that belong on the bottom scale.

5

Page 115

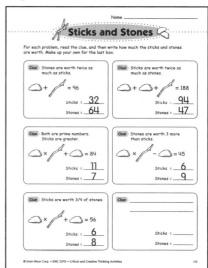

Sticks and Stones

For each problem, read the clue, and then write how much the sticks and stones are worth. Make up your own for the last box.

Clue: Stones are worth twice as much as sticks.
🪨 + 🪵 = 96
Sticks = **32**
Stones = **64**

Clue: Sticks are worth twice as much as stones.
🪵 + 🪨 + 🪵 = 188
Sticks = **94**
Stones = **47**

Clue: Both are prime numbers. Sticks are greater.
🪨 × 🪵 + 🪨 = 84
Sticks = **11**
Stones = **7**

Clue: Stones are worth 3 more than sticks.
🪵 × 🪨 − 🪨 = 45
Sticks = **6**
Stones = **9**

Clue: Sticks are worth 3/4 of stones.
🪨 × 🪵 + 🪨 = 56
Sticks = **6**
Stones = **8**

Clue: _____
Sticks = _____
Stones = _____

Page 116

Brothers and Sisters

Pretend that you are part of a large family with 6 brothers and 6 sisters. Fill in the chart with 3 advantages and 3 disadvantages of living in such a large family.

Advantages	Disadvantages

If it were up to you, would you be the oldest, the youngest, or an only child?

_____ Why? _____

Make 4-letter words by using 2 letters from each of the words BROTHER and SISTER. Example: toss

Possible answers include:

best	tote	tire	hose
rose	tore	site	riot
here	beet	boss	test
this	trot	rest	tier

Write a sentence about brothers or sisters. Use exactly 8 words.

_____

Page 117

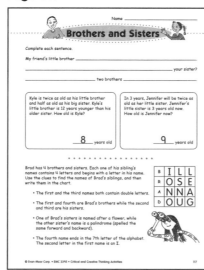

Brothers and Sisters

Complete each sentence.

My friend's little brother _____
_____ your sister?
_____ two brothers

Kyle is twice as old as his little brother and half as old as his big sister. Kyle's little brother is 12 years younger than his older sister. How old is Kyle?

8 years old

In 3 years, Jennifer will be twice as old as her little sister. Jennifer's little sister is 3 years old now. How old is Jennifer now?

9 years old

Brad has 4 brothers and sisters. Each one of his sibling's names contains 4 letters and begins with a letter in his name. Use the clues to find the names of Brad's siblings, and then write them in the chart.

B I L L
R O S E
A N N A
D O U G

• The first and the third names both contain double letters.
• The first and fourth names are Brad's brothers while the second and third are his sisters.
• One of Brad's sisters is named after a flower, while the other sister's name is a palindrome (spelled the same forward and backward).
• The fourth name ends in the 7th letter of the alphabet. The second letter in the first name is an I.

Page 118

Brothers and Sisters

There are 6 brothers and sisters in the Johnson family. Use the clues to find out how old each sibling is and in what month each one was born. Make an X in a square when it cannot be an answer. Draw a circle when it is a correct answer. Hint: When you draw a circle in a square, you can make an X in all of the other squares in that row and column.

| | | Ages | | | | | Months Born | | | | |
		5 years old	6 years old	8 years old	10 years old	11 years old	14 years old	January	April	June	October	November
Siblings	Paul		○									○
	Carly							○	○			
	John				○				○		○	
	Tina	○								○	○	
	George			○						○		
	Janice					○		○				

1. John and Janice were both born in months that begin with the same letter as their names.
2. George's age is a double digit. It is also the same number as the month he was born in.
3. The twins are both girls.
4. The boy who is eight years old was born in November.
5. The oldest child is a boy. He was born in the sixth month of the year.

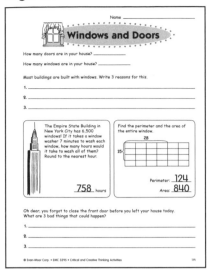

Windows and Doors

How many doors are in your house? _____

How many windows are in your house? _____

Most buildings are built with windows. Write 3 reasons for this.

1. _____
2. _____
3. _____

The Empire State Building in New York City has 6,500 windows! If it takes a window washer 7 minutes each to wash all of them, how many hours would it take to wash all of them? Round to the nearest hour.

758 hours

Find the perimeter and the area of the entire window.

Perimeter: **124**
Area: **840**

Oh dear, you forgot to close the front door before you left your house today. What are 3 bad things that could happen?

1. _____
2. _____
3. _____

Windows and Doors

Besides buildings, what are 5 other things that have doors?

1. _____
2. _____
3. _____
4. _____
5. _____

Windows are transparent. What are 5 other things that are transparent?

1. _____
2. _____
3. _____
4. _____
5. _____

What are 5 things you can see when you look out your bedroom window?

1. _____
2. _____
3. _____
4. _____
5. _____

When someone steps through the door to your house, what is the first thing you think he or she notices?

_____

Julia closed the window before she pulled the curtains. She let the cat out before she locked the door. She locked the door before she closed the window. In what order did Julia do those 4 things?

First: **let cat out**
Second: **locked door**
Third: **closed window**
Fourth: **pulled curtains**

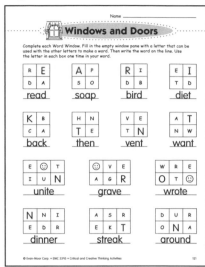

Windows and Doors

Complete each Word Window. Fill in the empty window pane with a letter that can be used with the other letters to make a word. Then write the word on the line. Use the letter in each box one time in your word.

read   soap   bird   diet

back   then   vent   want

unite   grave   wrote

dinner streak around

Read All About It!

What are 5 ways your life would be harder if you could not read?

1. _____
2. _____
3. _____
4. _____
5. _____

Number the things from 1 to 10 according to how much you would like to read them. The thing you would like to read the most should be number 1.

_____ newspaper
_____ scary story
_____ encyclopedia
_____ classic novel
_____ history book
_____ back of a cereal box
_____ magazine
_____ chapter book
_____ friend's web page
_____ biography

Ken has a goal to read one million words this year. If each page contains about 250 words, about how many pages will he need to read to attain his goal?

4,000 pages

If the books Ken reads are about 200 pages long, how many books will he read?

20 books

Read All About It!

Sometimes books are made into movies (for example, *Charlotte's Web* or *Harry Potter*). Make a ✓ by the one you would rather do. Then write why on the lines.

☐ read the book first, and then see the movie
☐ see the movie first, and then read the book
☐ just read the book
☐ just see the movie

Why? _____

What was the last book that you read? _____

Write 3 words to describe that book. _____

Summarize the book in one sentence. _____

How good was the book? Rate it by filling in 1 to 5 stars. ☆☆☆☆☆

What are the 5 best books you have ever read?

1. _____
2. _____
3. _____
4. _____
5. _____

Logan read 75 books last year. 40 percent of them were about animals. How many animal books did Logan read last year?

30 animal books

Read All About It!

Each book in the stacks below was written by someone whose name has something to do with what he or she wrote about. Match the authors to the books by writing the correct number in the box next to each title.

1. Brock Lee   5. Robin Banks   9. Liza Woke   13. Bill Ding
2. Dan Saul Knight   6. Ima Painter   10. Ray King   14. Nick L. Andime
3. Dinah Sorus   7. Vic Tory   11. Marcus Absent   15. Alec Tricity
4. Joe Kerr   8. Mel Ting   12. Ira Fuse   16. Izzy Backyet

Great Artists **6**
Under Construction **13**
Prehistoric Giants **3**
Learn to Say "No" **12**
Learn to Tango **2**
Biography of a Comedian **4**
A Shocking Tale **15**
The Long Trip **16**

Crime Doesn't Pay **5**
The Long Hot Summer **8**
Be a Winner **7**
Cooking Vegetables **1**
Curing Insomnia **9**
Money Management **14**
Playing Hooky **11**
Yardwork for Dummies **10**

Screen Time

Would you rather watch TV or use the computer? _____
Why? _____

Number the kinds of TV shows from 1 to 8 according to how much you would want to watch them. The one you want to watch the most should be number 1.

_____ cooking show
_____ news
_____ game show
_____ sitcom
_____ cartoon
_____ nature program
_____ talk show
_____ reality show

During September, Katie used the computer for 45 minutes each day. During October, she used the computer for an hour each day. How many more hours did she use the computer in October than in September?

8½ hours

What is your favorite TV show?
_____

About how much TV do you watch each week? _____
How much TV do you think a person your age should watch each week? _____
Why? _____

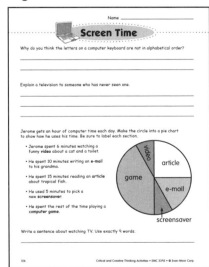

Screen Time

Why do you think the letters on a computer keyboard are not in alphabetical order?

_____

Explain a television to someone who has never seen one.

_____

Jerome gets an hour of computer time each day. Make the circle into a pie chart to show how he uses his time. Be sure to label each section.

- Jerome spent 6 minutes watching a funny video about a cat and a toilet.
- He spent 10 minutes writing an e-mail to his grandma.
- He spent 15 minutes reading an article about tropical fish.
- He used 5 minutes to pick a new screensaver.
- He spent the rest of the time playing a computer game.

video article game e-mail screensaver

Write a sentence about watching TV. Use exactly 9 words.

_____

Screen Time

The left side of the chart below lists the top 20 TV shows for last week. In the center are some clues about where the shows ranked this week. Use the clues to list this week's top 20 TV shows on the right side of the chart.

TOP 20 SHOWS		This Week
Clue	Rank	Show
Down 2	1	Dancing with Dopey
Down 8	2	560 Minutes
Even number < 14	3	American I-Sore
Up 4	4	The Last-Night Show
Up 1	5	What Not to Eat
Odd number > 11	6	Slugs in the City
Up 5	7	The Rachel L Show
Prime number > 7	8	Flint 48501
Down 5	9	Saturday Night Llamas
Up 4	10	Name That Pickle
Tens • ones = 9	11	List Busters
Prime number < 6	12	Gilligan's Toothpaste
Down 7	13	Bowling for Furniture
Up 3	14	The Obstructed View
Symmetrical	15	Dr. Empty
Nearly last	16	America's Funniest Hats
Up 10	17	Desperate House Cats
Tens • ones = 8	18	Trading Faces
Even number	19	Project Runway
Odd number	20	Extreme Homework

Critical and Creative Thinking Activities • EMC 3395 • © Evan-Moor Corp.

Page 128

Page 129

Page 130

Page 131

Page 132

Page 133

Page 134

Page 135

Page 136

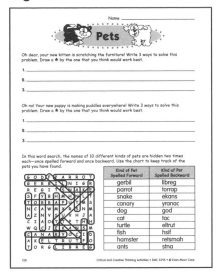

Page 128 — Pets

Name _____

Oh dear, your new kitten is scratching the furniture! Write 3 ways to solve this problem. Draw a ★ by the one that you think would work best.

1. _____
2. _____
3. _____

Oh no! Your new puppy is making puddles everywhere! Write 3 ways to solve this problem. Draw a ★ by the one that you think would work best.

1. _____
2. _____
3. _____

In this word search, the names of 10 different kinds of pets are hidden two times each—once spelled forward and once backward. Use the chart to keep track of the pets you have found.

Kind of Pet Spelled Forward	Kind of Pet Spelled Backward
gerbil	libreg
parrot	torrap
snake	ekans
canary	yranac
dog	god
cat	tac
turtle	eltrut
fish	hsif
hamster	retsmah
ants	stna

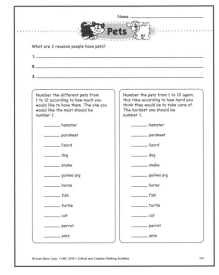

Page 129 — Pets

Name _____

What are 3 reasons people have pets?

1. _____
2. _____
3. _____

Number the different pets from 1 to 12 according to how much you would like to have them. The one you would like the most should be number 1.

_____ hamster
_____ parakeet
_____ lizard
_____ dog
_____ snake
_____ guinea pig
_____ horse
_____ fish
_____ turtle
_____ cat
_____ parrot
_____ ants

Number the pets from 1 to 12 again, this time according to how hard you think they would be to take care of. The hardest one should be number 1.

_____ hamster
_____ parakeet
_____ lizard
_____ dog
_____ snake
_____ guinea pig
_____ horse
_____ fish
_____ turtle
_____ cat
_____ parrot
_____ ants

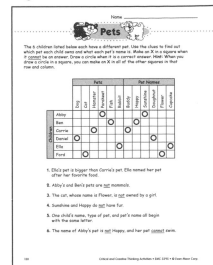

Page 130 — Pets

Name _____

The 6 children listed below each have a different pet. Use the clues to find out which pet each child owns and what each pet's name is. Make an X in a square when it cannot be an answer. Draw a circle when it is a correct answer. Hint: When you draw a circle in a square, you can make an X in all of the other squares in that row and column.

1. Ella's pet is bigger than Carrie's pet. Ella named her pet after her favorite food.
2. Abby's and Ben's pets are not mammals.
3. The cat, whose name is Flower, is not owned by a girl.
4. Sunshine and Happy do not have fur.
5. One child's name, type of pet, and pet's name all begin with the same letter.
6. The name of Abby's pet is not Happy, and her pet cannot swim.

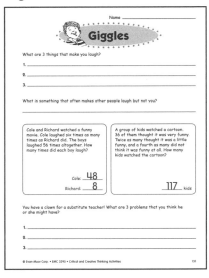

Page 131 — Giggles

Name _____

What are 3 things that make you laugh?

1. _____
2. _____
3. _____

What is something that often makes other people laugh but not you?

_____

Cole and Richard watched a funny movie. Cole laughed six times as many times as Richard did. The boys laughed 56 times altogether. How many times did each boy laugh?

Cole: **48**
Richard: **8**

A group of kids watched a cartoon. 36 of them thought it was very funny. Twice as many thought it was a little funny, and a fourth of that did not think it was funny at all. How many kids watched the cartoon?

117 kids

You have a clown for a substitute teacher! What are 3 problems that you think he or she might have?

1. _____
2. _____
3. _____

Page 132 — Giggles

Name _____

Fill in the blanks with words to make each sentence funny.

One day, _____ frog jumped into a big _____

My mother always says I should never _____ with my _____

The boys were late for _____ because they _____

Use the clues to find things that can be funny. Cross out the letters you use on the right. Then unscramble the remaining letters to make a word that means the same thing as giggle.

big shoes, red nose — **clown**
animated TV show — **cartoon**
checked out at the library — **book**
in the newspaper — **comics**
in a theater or on DVD — **movie**
tell one to a friend — **joke**

Letters left: **HUKLCEC**

Another word for giggle is: **chuckle**

What do they have in common?

Lucy, Calvin, Garfield: **comic-strip characters**
Banana peel, wet floor, soap: **slippery**
Pilkey, Dahl, Seuss: **authors**

Write a funny sentence that has 6 words in it.

_____

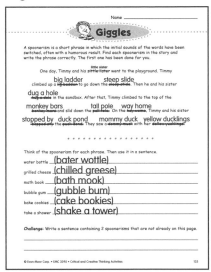

Page 133 — Giggles

Name _____

A spoonerism is a short phrase in which the initial sounds of the words have been switched, often with a humorous result. Find each spoonerism in the story and write the phrase correctly. The first one has been done for you.

little sister
One day, Timmy and his ~~sittle lister~~ went to the playground. Timmy
big ladder   steep slide
climbed up a ~~lig badder~~ to go down the ~~sleep slide~~. Then he and his sister
dug a hole
~~hug a dole~~ in the sandbox. After that, Timmy climbed to the top of the
monkey bars   tall pole   way home
~~donkey mars~~ and slid down the ~~pall tole~~. On the ~~hay wome~~, Timmy and his sister
stopped by   duck pond   mommy duck   yellow ducklings
~~stopped dy~~ the ~~puck dond~~. They saw a ~~dommy muck~~ with her ~~dellow yucklings~~.

Think of the spoonerism for each phrase. Then use it in a sentence.

water bottle — **(bater wottle)**
grilled cheese — **(chilled greese)**
math book — **(bath mook)**
bubble gum — **(gubble bum)**
bake cookies — **(cake bookies)**
take a shower — **(shake a tower)**

Challenge: Write a sentence containing 2 spoonerisms that are not already on this page.

Page 134 — Emotions

Name _____

What would make you feel...

happy? _____
frustrated? _____
nervous? _____
proud? _____

What are 6 ways you can make yourself feel better when you are feeling sad?

1. _____
2. _____
3. _____
4. _____
5. _____
6. _____

Claudia, Jamie, and Basil each made a list of things that make them happy. Jamie's list was 3 times as long as Basil's list. Claudia's list was half as long as Jamie's List. Together, Jamie's and Basil's lists were 120 things long. How long was each child's list?

Claudia: **45**
Jamie: **90**
Basil: **30**

SIMILES
My mom was as angry as _____
Our teacher was as surprised as _____
The fear I felt was like _____
The little boy was as sad as _____

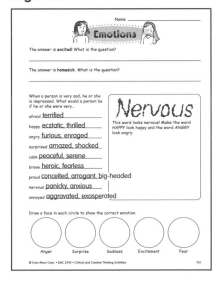

Page 135 — Emotions

Name _____

The answer is excited! What is the question?

_____

The answer is homesick. What is the question?

_____

When a person is very sad, he or she is depressed. What would a person be if he or she were very...

afraid — **terrified**
happy — **ecstatic, thrilled**
angry — **furious, enraged**
surprised — **amazed, shocked**
calm — **peaceful, serene**
brave — **heroic, fearless**
proud — **conceited, arrogant, big-headed**
nervous — **panicky, anxious**
annoyed — **aggravated, exasperated**

Nervous
This word looks nervous! Make the word HAPPY look happy and the word ANGRY look angry.

Draw a face in each circle to show the correct emotion.

Anger   Surprise   Sadness   Excitement   Fear

Page 136 — Emotions

Name _____

Can you think of a way you could feel for each letter of the alphabet? Try to write words for at least 20 of the letters.

Answers will vary.
Accept any appropriate responses.

C_____   P_____
D_____   Q_____
E_____   R_____
F_____   S_____
G_____   T_____
H_____   U_____
I_____   V_____
J_____   W_____
K_____   EX_____
L_____   Y_____
M_____   Z_____

Choose one of the emotions above and write it on the line. Then use it to make as many smaller words as you can.

1. _____   9. _____
2. _____   10. _____
3. _____   11. _____
4. _____   12. _____
5. _____
6. _____
7. _____
8. _____

Page 137

Name _____

Choices

Every day, you make dozens of choices: what to wear, what to eat, where to sit. How many choices do you think you have made today? _____

What are 3 of those choices?

1. _____
2. _____
3. _____

Kristin has decided to paint every room in her house. She has chosen a different color of paint for each room. Read the clues and write the name of the color (blue, green, yellow, purple, or orange) she has picked for each room.

- The kitchen and the dining room are both primary colors.
- The bedroom is *not* orange.
- The colors of the dining room and the living room are both one-syllable words.

Kitchen: **yellow**
Dining room: **blue**
Living room: **green**
Bathroom: **orange**
Bedroom: **purple**

What is one of the most important choices you have ever made?

_____

What do you think will be 2 of the most important choices you'll make in the future?

1. _____
2. _____

© Evan-Moor Corp. • EMC 3395 • Critical and Creative Thinking Activities   137

Page 138

Name _____

Choices

Choose one word for each pair and circle it.

elephant or frog   table or chair   big or small   pen or crayon

Now write one sentence using all 4 of the words that you circled.

_____

Try this fun math game!

Choose any number. _____

Add 3. _____

Multiply your result by 10. _____

Multiply your result by your original number. _____

Subtract 10. _____

Divide by 10. _____

Add 1. _____

Divide by your original number. _____

Subtract 3 from the number. _____

Subtract your original number. _____

If you got 0, you did it right!

There are 4 different kinds of cookies in the big cookie jar. Each child chooses 3 different kinds of cookies. How many different combinations are possible?

4 cookie combinations

What can you do if your friend makes an important choice that you do not agree with?

_____

138   Critical and Creative Thinking Activities • EMC 3395 • © Evan-Moor Corp.

Page 139

Name _____

Choices

Choose one, and then tell why you picked it.

Would you rather...

be a monkey or a hawk? _____
Why? _____

be a pencil or a stapler? _____
Why? _____

be an ice-cream bar or a carrot? _____
Why? _____

be able to turn invisible or to fly? _____
Why? _____

be super smart or super good-looking? _____
Why? _____

live for the rest of your life without TV or without junk food? _____
Why? _____

be good in school or good at sports? _____
Why? _____

© Evan-Moor Corp. • EMC 3395 • Critical and Creative Thinking Activities   139

Page 140

Name _____

Homework

About how much homework do you do each day? _____

Do you think that amount is too much, too little, or about right? _____

Why do you think so? _____

Charlotte can do 1 math problem in a minute and a half. There are 36 math problems on the homework page, but Charlotte has been assigned *only* the even-numbered ones. How long will it take her to complete her homework?

27 minutes

Thomas started his homework at 7:43. At 8:18, he took an 8-minute break to have a snack. He finished his homework at 8:39. How long did Thomas spend doing homework?

48 minutes

Krystal did her homework, but she did not turn it in. What are 3 possible reasons?

1. _____
2. _____
3. _____

Write a sentence using the words *homework, pencil, easy,* and *goat.*

_____

140   Critical and Creative Thinking Activities • EMC 3395 • © Evan-Moor Corp.

Page 141

Name _____

Homework

You get to assign your class homework today, but you <u>must</u> follow these rules:

- The assignment you give should take about as long as your usual homework does.
- It must involve paper and a pen or pencil.
- It must be challenging.

Subject: _____   Homework assignment: _____

What would your classmates learn from doing this assignment?

_____

● ● ● ● ● ● ● ● ● ● ● ● ● ● ● ● ●

What kind of homework does Benjamin have tonight? Follow the directions and rewrite the word on each new line until you find it out.

Directions	B	E	N	J	A	M	I	N
Make the third letter the same as the second letter.	B	E	E	J	A	M	I	N
Change the sixth letter to the vowel that is in both *STRAIGHT* and *STRIKE.*	B	E	E	J	A	I	I	N
Change the first letter to the letter that comes before T in the alphabet.	S	E	E	J	A	I	I	N
Change the last letter to the seventh letter in the alphabet.	S	E	E	J	A	I	I	G
Change the fourth and fifth letters to L.	S	E	E	L	L	I	I	G
Change the seventh letter to the letter that is in both *PENCIL* and *GROWN.*	S	E	E	L	L	I	N	G
Change the second letter to the letter that comes before Q in the alphabet.	S	P	E	L	L	I	N	G

© Evan-Moor Corp. • EMC 3395 • Critical and Creative Thinking Activities   141

Page 142

Name _____

Homework

Homework is a compound word. Find your way through the puzzle below by forming compound words from one box to the next. You may move up, down, or across, but *not* diagonally. Start with *HOME* in the upper-left corner and end with *LAND* in the lower-right corner.

HOME	RUN	WAY	WRONG	BLUE	GREEN	APPLE	BEST
WORK	OUT	SIDE	HAPPY	FACE	OFF	PIE	FRIEND
HARD	KEY	LINE	DOWN	TOWN	HALL	HOME	SHIP
UP	HOLE	UP	STAIRS	LIGHT	SWITCH	PLATE	COUNT
TOP	HAT	HOLD	OVER	NIGHT	MARE	COLT	HOOF
TEA	SPOON	MIX	GOAT	STAND	UP	CHUCK	IN
CUP	SEE	MATCH	COOLER	OFF	THERE	PAPER	ROCK
RED	FREE	FALL	WATER	SPRING	TIME	SHARE	OUT
CLOUD	BURST	BACK	FRONT	SUN	BEAM	WARE	SHIRT
BIRD	BLACK	PACK	RAT	BOOK	CASE	PHONE	HOME
WING	SHOE	HORSE	POWER	HOUSE	BREAK	DOWN	FRONT
TALL	SHINE	ON	LIGHT	BOAT	OUT	TURN	ABOUT
TREE	HILL	TOP	OUT	HAND	OFF	OVER	COMIC
HOUSE	DOOR	KNOB	SIDE	WAYS	SHIRT	STOCK	BOOK
GRASS	MAT	RUG	BOX	CAR	OPEN	YARD	SALE
CART	WHEEL	TUG	BOY	POOL	HOUSE	STICK	BALL
ANT	MINT	BOAT	BUBBLE	GUM	FILE	WAY	PARK
HILL	BAR	MAN	KIND	MEAL	WORK	SNACK	LAND

142   Critical and Creative Thinking Activities • EMC 3395 • © Evan-Moor Corp.

Critical and Creative Thinking Activities • EMC 3395 • © Evan-Moor Corp.

Evan-Moor's
Daily Plan & Daily Record Books

Two must-have teacher resources with three fun themes to choose from!

Daily Plan Books

Organize your entire school year—and with style! Original artwork brings a touch of fun to these spiral-bound planners. 96 pages.

Daily Plan Book: School Days
All Grades   EMC 5400

Daily Plan Book: Garden Days
All Grades   EMC 5401

Daily Plan Book: Animal Academy
All Grades   EMC 5402

Animal Academy

School Days

Garden Days

Daily Record Books

Finally, all the forms you need to track and record student progress in one spot! 96 pages.

Daily Record Book: School Days
All Grades   EMC 5403

Daily Record Book: Garden Days
All Grades   EMC 5404

Daily Record Book: Animal Academy
All Grades   EMC 5405

Must-have resources that make learning fun!

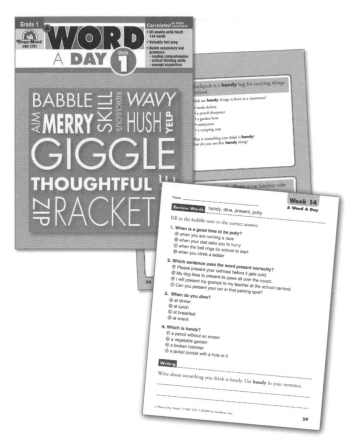

A Word a Day

Help your students develop the rich and diverse vocabulary they need for academic success!

Research shows that strong vocabulary and word knowledge is directly linked to academic accomplishment. Make sure your students develop the rich vocabulary that's essential to successful reading comprehension and academic achievement with *A Word a Day*. Each book in this newly revised series covers 144 words in 36 engaging weekly units. And with new features, such as an oral review and a written assessment for each week, it's easier than ever to help your students develop the vocabulary they need.

Correlated to state standards and Common Core State Standards.

Grade 1	EMC 2791
Grade 2	EMC 2792
Grade 3	EMC 2793
Grade 4	EMC 2794
Grade 5	EMC 2795
Grade 6+	EMC 2796

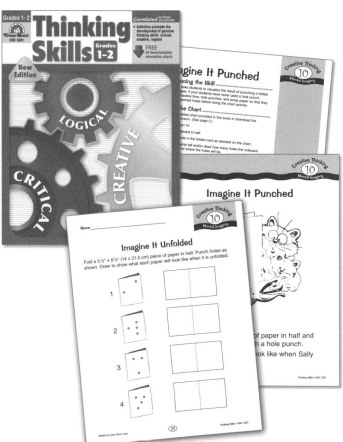

Thinking Skills

Help your students practice thinking skills with the creative and engaging activities in the *Thinking Skills* series. The 44 imaginative lessons in each book include downloadable interactive charts and reproducible practice pages to help your students think creatively, logically, and critically.

Correlated to state standards and Common Core State Standards.

Grades 1–2	EMC 5301
Grades 3–4	EMC 5302
Grades 5–6	EMC 5303